CULTIVATING

PEACE

Receiving God's Peace Within Your Chaos

STEPHANIE HAYNES

Table of Contents

Foreword

It was the day of my daughter's second birthday. As usual on party day, things were chaotic...I was running late and still had a million things to do before I pulled off the *perfect* birthday party. I was dragging my birthday girl from place to place, running errands for the big event. As we drove down the road, the whining started. First, as a soft complaint, but quickly escalating...the same as my blood pressure. Before I knew it, I whipped around in the seat of our van and popped her leg. Instant shame flooded me. I pulled the van over and apologized and cuddled her until she calmed down.

My home looked perfect for the party. Nothing was out of place. I had great appetizers for the adults, perfect goody bags for the kids, fun games and lots of perfectly staged pictures. But what lay underneath was an exhausted husband who had worked tirelessly to help me pull it off, an exhausted child who didn't really like crowds and being the center of attention, and a worn out mom who was way too concerned with appearances; a worn out mom who had her priorities all out of order.

Then I met Stephanie. She was teaching a small group called "Cultivating Peace" at Seacoast Church in Mt. Pleasant, SC. Just the name of the study sold me! Peace is what I craved. At that time, there was no book yet, just handouts and Stephanie leading class. I was hooked. She introduced the idea of what God's order for our lives looked like and how it was possible to follow that order in a practical (and peace-filled) way. As we finished that class, I knew I needed more. I approached her about taking the class again. I still needed to hear it once more and have it cemented in my head. It turns out once more wasn't enough, and I have followed Stephanie as she has turned those handouts and lectures into a book that has been through 2 additional rewrites as God continues to refine His message to women all over the United States.

My daughter is now 18 and those days of super-woman-wanna-be-must-be-perfect days are long gone. Now I strive to 1) keep God first in all things, 2) keep myself filled with His love, 3) keep my marriage healthy and build up my husband, 4) train my kids in the way they should go – yes even at 18, 5)and lastly (which used to be #1!) keeping my home and work-peace-filled not perfect...peace-filled.

Stephanie has a way with words that could only be God-given. She has taught thousands of women how to live a peace-filled life in a chaotic world using practical steps and examples from her own life. This new revision of Cultivating Peace is her best one yet. As God continues to refine her story and teach her, she passes on those nuggets of wisdom in this latest re-vision. I am a different woman because of her willingness to obey God and put his priorities for our lives into words that make sense and echo the real life struggles we face as women, wives, mothers and employees.

Stephanie has become my friend, mentor, and biggest cheerleader in life. I will continue to teach this bible study every year probably for the rest of my life. Cultivating Peace is a game changer so be ready for the greatest adventure of your life!

Lorin Tinder

Acknowledgements

This book would not have come together without the amazing grace of God. He alone took all the chaos of my life and used it to bring me closer to Him. It is so true that He uses *all things for the good of those who love Him, who have been called according to his purpose!* (Romans 8:28)

To my husband: Thank you. I am the woman, wife, and mother I am today because of you. Your patience, unconditional love, and encouragement have been the greatest gifts you have given me. May God continue to bless our marriage and grow us closer to Him until we meet Him face-to-face.

To my children: Thank you. You are the reason I share my story. My life of chaos has value, but I want so much more than that for you both. I hope you know how much I respect and love you. May God bless you both with a rich and satisfying relationship with Himself.

To my Tribe (You know who you are): You women! Do you know how incredible you are? Self-sacrificing, grace-filled, truth-tellers, all of you. You have held my arms up when I didn't think I could follow Jesus any deeper. You have shed light on the steps I couldn't see. You have given life and meaning to the struggles I have faced, and taught me how to open the doors of my heart to let God's restoration in. Thank you.

Note from the Author

The material in this book is revised and updated from the original Cultivating Peace: Revealing God's Peace within Your Chaos. As I have learned and grown in my life's journey, I have come to understand grace in a much deeper capacity. Grace is unmerited favor; God blessing us despite the fact that we do not deserve it. I have learned that God knows we will mess up and does not hold us to a perfect standard to way the world does. In grace we have freedom to live a messy life without fear of losing His love. Previous versions focused mainly on teaching how to maintain peace through our own actions.

What I have learned is that peace comes when we choose to allow Jesus' leadership of our lives to dictate the when's, how's, and what's of our lives, not our own expectations or the expectations of the culture in which we live. It is a messy process, filled with mistakes, which is why grace is so important. When we can remember that God is truly in control of everything in our lives, we are free to take courageous steps of faith no matter how messy they become. God is with us, every step, and wants us to be successful. All He asks is for a willing heart.

Introduction

From Chaos to Peace

"Trust in the Lord with all your heart; do
not depend on your own understanding.
Seek his will in all you do, and
He will show you which path to take."

Proverbs 3:5-6 NLT

Introduction

I grew up believing I could do whatever I set my mind to. And for the most part, I achieved everything I set out to do. I was one of those "Type A," gotta-do-it-all-perfectly type of women. The result was a life so chaotic that I was a wreck. How crazy was I from wanting to have it all? In the ten years between graduation from high school and the birth of my first child

- I crammed as many units into each semester at college so I could earn my BA and Secondary Teaching Credentials in four and a half years.

- I worked continually throughout college, holding down two full-time jobs over the summer, in addition to a part-time job during the school year.

- I became a full-time high school English teacher and led the Technology Committee, the Student Academic Recognition Committee (Renaissance), and the Accreditation Committee. Additionally, I was the coach of the cheerleading squad and the co-chair of the English department.

- I held down additional jobs over summer breaks and holidays.

- I got married to my college sweetheart.

- I became pregnant with my daughter.

I was a busy woman to be sure, but I believed I could hold it all together if I could only make things "just right" in my life. I tried organizing my time well. I made schedules, to-do lists, and streamlined as much as I could. Once I got married and my daughter was born, I read every article I could find on managing a household as an equal partnership between working parents. I tried to do everything they said while desperately wanting my emotionally and physically withdrawn husband to pitch in. When mommy-guilt poured in (which was almost every day), I did what I could to spend more time with my daughter; but there was always so much to do. I always felt as if I was trying to manage a whirlwind.

Even though life was crazy then, some of my most chaotic days were still on the horizon. During the three years after our daughter was born, while I continued to teach high school full-time, my husband and I went through a difficult period in our marriage and almost divorced. I also conceived again, but our pregnancy ended in a miscarriage. I was confused, lonely, disillusioned, and hurt. Career, marriage, and motherhood had completely overwhelmed me to the point that I didn't know how I could go on if things didn't change.

Knowing that things need to change, but not knowing how to do it, can be a very frustrating place to be. That's exactly where I was when God stepped in.

I had known my whole life that there was a God, but because of several circumstances He had not been an important part of most of my life to that point. But, I had made a friend, and she knew God. As I got to know her she seemed to handle the storms of motherhood, working, and being married so much better than I. So when she invited me to church I decided to go and check this whole "God-thing" out.

> "Knowing that things need to change, but not knowing how to do it, can be a very frustrating place to be."

While there was an intense longing in my heart for joy, peace, and safety, each Sunday morning I attended church I left feeling conflicted; I wanted peace but I still wasn't so sure this "God-thing" was for me. It seemed scary to trade the known, no matter how crazy it was, for the unknown.

During that time, my husband and I committed to working through our issues and were able to learn to love each other enough that I conceived and gave birth to our son. It was during my pregnancy however that my husband was awarded a promotion that would forever change our lives. I should have been thrilled, but the promotion came with two devastating catches: we would have to move out of the state in which we had spent our whole lives, and I would have to give up my teaching career.

As I sat in bed one morning, two months after my son was born, I was fully confronted with the fact that I would soon be leaving everything and everyone I had ever known. I realized I would be trading my hometown in the Bay Area of California for the strange land of Mount Pleasant, South Carolina. I was overwhelmed and terrified. I had also been reading the first book in the "Left Behind" series by Tim

LaHaye and Jerry B. Jenkins. The characters in that book were overwhelmed and terrified as well and I had identified with them. The authors had offered a prayer at the front of the book and instructions for those seeking a relationship with God through Jesus Christ. In the midst of my meltdown that morning, I got on my knees, read that prayer aloud with conviction in my heart that this was my last option, hoped life would get better, and invited Jesus to live in my heart forever.

Though that may have been the beginning of a new spiritual life, my body and emotions were still in a state of turmoil. After my son was born I began wearing a heart monitor twenty-four hours a day to track my heart's rhythm because it had been behaving erratically (due to a heart murmur that was caused by stress). I learned the weekend I moved into my new house in Mount Pleasant, South Carolina that my dad had lung cancer (He passed away ten short months later, in California). Adding to that, one month later I rolled our SUV into a ditch with my kids and husband in it. The last straw came when, as the result of several "unexplained" symptoms, I was tested and found to be in stress-induced perimenopause.

Due to my increased stress level, my doctor suggested I see a counselor who explained that in less than one year I had experienced all the major causes of depression: leaving a career, moving to a new place, having a baby, beginning a new career (I was now a stay-at-home mom), getting in a car accident, and dealing with the loss of a loved one. I was of no use to anyone and felt as if I was in a constant state of emotional turmoil.

The question that always haunted the back of my mind was: *"What's wrong with me?"* I had given my life to Jesus. I had found a church in our new hometown and attended regularly. I served in the children's ministry and as a small group leader for our women's ministry. I participated in my daughter's school activities (she was in elementary school by this time). I tried to do everything "right." Why was there no relief? The joy, peace, and safety I was looking for still eluded me.

Through it all I would spend time daily talking to God, but nothing seemed to get any better. I would sit in church begging God to fix all my problems, to give me some relief from all the stress I was under, only to walk out and feel the weight of it all sink right back onto my shoulders again. Hopelessness crept into my heart and my depression grew worse.

Thankfully, God knew I needed His help. In October of 2005 as I was once again pouring out my heart to God asking Him to fix my life, I felt the words *"Be still and know that I am God"* (Psalm 46:10 NIV) being spoken directly into my heart, but I didn't understand. I was still so steeped in trying to be in control of my life that I actually said back, "That's impossible! How am I supposed to *"Be still"* with a seven-year-old, a three-year-old, church commitments, a house to run, and everything else I have to do?"

In response to my frustrations, God directed me to Jeremiah 29:11, *"For I know the plans I have for you…plans to prosper you and not to harm you, plans to give you hope and a future."* My reaction? Stubborn obstinacy. I told God that if He had such great plans for me, if He wanted me to *"Be still,"* He was going to have to figure it out for me.

Out of His vast love for me, God began clearing out my schedule. Bible study groups I was participating in ended without any follow-up studies to replace it. Then, my daughter's school suddenly didn't need me to help out. At this point I figured God was really trying to get my attention, so I began to cooperate. I looked for other ways to clear out my schedule so I could *"Be still..."* I asked a friend to work out a carpool for my son's preschool. I began to make menus and errand schedules and stopped running out to shop every day. I stopped trying to fix up my home and instead focused on just keeping it picked up.

I suddenly found myself with free time on my hands, and for the first time ever I had no plan. So, I became still and asked God to tell me what He was up to. He nowhad my full attention. What He showed me has changed my life.

God Reveals His Plan

Have you ever thought you had it all figured out, only to realize you were horribly off track? That's what I felt as I sat one morning in my kitchen, trying to *"Be still,"* wondering how I had arrived at a place where I was so stressed out my physical body and my emotional stability were both in jeopardy. I had tried to do what was right all these years. I had sought to be a productive member of society. I had worked hard to take care of everyone and everything around me. Why, if I indeed had done what I was supposed to do, was my life such a mess?

The answer to that question came after allowing God to work out all the legalism I had been living with through reading the book of Ephesians in my Bible. (Legalism is the act of living by strict rules and expectations in order to earn love and acceptance.) It was the first encounter with reading the Bible I'd ever had. I spent months studying this letter on Christian living, looking up every notation so I could be sure I really understood. In that process, I became still enough to understand what it meant to know God and an awful, yet absolutely freeing, revelation dawned on me: my life was such a mess because I had tried to do *everything*, and tried to do it all on my own. I realized that it was my choice to run my life based on my own understanding that was causing all the trouble, but that I could choose to trust God's way instead.

That spring, during those three months I was learning what God meant by *"Be still,"* I noticed that something changed in me that I still can't quite describe. Paul describes it as being *"transformed by the renewing of your mind"* (Romans 12:12 NIV). All I can say is that this time of being still with God completely changed how I thought about things. I no longer ran around trying to get everything done. If there wasn't enough time, I waited until tomorrow instead of continuing my pattern of getting frustrated with those around me as I rushed through it all. I began looking for ways to take care of my family better, without resentment, rather than feeling bitter that no one was taking care of me. I didn't say yes to a request for my time immediately but rather intentionally chose where I was going to spend the time I had been given each day, which included taking care of myself. I began to see each day as an opportunity for peace rather than a time of chaos.

A friend noticed the positive results of the changes in my behaviors and, after questioning what was going on with me, decided I needed to tell other women what God was up to in my life. I wasn't so sure, though. High school students I can speak to all day long. Other adult women though were an audience of which I was terrified. Still, as any good friend would do, she pushed me out of my new-found comfort zone and right in front of the type of women I was especially terrified of: pastor's wives, small group leaders, and other faith-filled, deeply committed women in ministry.

While my friend was certain she was doing the right thing, I was terrified. What on earth could I possibly share with these powerhouse Christian women? I felt completely unworthy and overwhelmed. So, deep in prayer at my kitchen table one morning, I poured out my heart, pleading for the words to speak. As I sat waiting for God's wisdom to somehow appear on the blank pages in front of me, I noticed the view of my back porch through the window. While there is something in me that rejoices every time I plant a tree, pull weeds or plant flowers in a container, I hadn't made much time to garden in a while. As I looked out that window onto my back porch I noticed the container of petunias, impatiens, and pansies I had planted several months before was no longer vibrant and thriving, but dry, run-down, and over-grown with weeds.

In what I believe now was a divine-inspired vision, I felt God again whisper to me: *"That's what you were."* God imprinted the image of my dry, run-down, overgrown life before me. *"That isn't what I had planned for you. My plans are different."* My mind became flooded with images of all the things I had been doing with God over the previous months:

- I had developed a relationship with God through his Son Jesus Christ and made Him my number one priority, giving Him the first and best parts of my day.

- I had for the first time actually begun to listen to the stirrings of resting when I needed to, playing when I needed to, and taking care of myself.

- I had been intentional in taking more time to be with my husband instead of placing him last on my to-do list.

- I had been focusing on being with my children in their activities, rather than just moving them throughout my day.

- My home no longer stressed me out because the people within it had become much more important than making sure it was spotless.

- I had intentionally chosen which activities to be involved in that fit into my new schedule rather than letting all those outside obligations dictate the rest of my life.

As I sat there, in so many tears I almost couldn't see, I realized that as I had chosen to stop doing things my way, God had gently stepped in to lead. As a result, He had taken my life of chaos and replaced it with His peace. All of a sudden I had an overpowering thought. If you consider life in gardening terms, our lives are like the empty planter we use when we are planting a small container garden: **We all have a life, but it's what we choose to fill it with that makes all the difference.**

In gardening, if we want our plants to have the best chance of thriving, there is a pattern to filling the containers: rock at the base for good drainage, nourished soil to promote healthy development, and complimentary plants meant to thrive

"We all have a life but it's what we choose to fill it with that makes all the difference."

together. In addition, there's the after-planting care: watering, pruning, and adequate light and food. I realized that cultivating a peace-filled life follows a similar pattern. Begin with the Rock, Jesus Christ, as our foundation, infuse our lives with the truth of God's nourishing Word, and allow the Holy Spirit to lead us each day.

Taking care to live a peace-centered life follows a pattern also. Water daily by listening to the promptings of the Holy Spirit in how to spend the time we are given each day, prune activities and even relationships when necessary to keep from overcrowding our schedules, bask in the grace of Jesus daily, and refresh ourselves with the Word of God as we face life's struggles.

I took that lesson and shared it with those powerhouse women that night, filled with trepidation. Would they love it? Would they think I was crazy? Would it be enough?

The result of that 20-minute lesson is this book you are reading. Over the weeks and months after that presentation, I was asked to share my story again and again. What began as a small presentation morphed into several weeks of instruction to hundreds of women under the care and guidance of the pastors at our church.[1] In that time, I realized that all the issues I had faced over the past few years, both physically and emotionally, God was now using for His glory. All the stressful situations, the busy schedules, the failures at trying to make everything perfect, I now saw as lessons of God's grace.

I finally understood that the pathway to peace required that I stop trying to be in control and instead allow God's plans to prevail.

When I left that evening I was changed. I was no longer the woman who had suffered needlessly in chaos for years: **I was a woman who had been given the gift of peace because of the chaos**. A new purpose was being cultivated in my heart: to teach women how to receive God's peace, no matter how chaotic the circumstance, through grace-filled instruction in how to trust God at His Word.

What to do With This Book

The process I have undergone *began* with that season of being still before God. Since then it has been an incredible journey that is constantly evolving and growing in ways I could never have imagined. In this book, I am sharing what worked for me as a result of my obedience to trusting His way over my own. While I believe that the principles I share are sound, I maintain that your journey will look very different from mine. My life is different from yours, and that's how it's supposed to be. We are not meant to be carbon-copies of each other and I do not want to make you believe in any way that we should live our lives in the same way. While I believe that God does have an order as to how we treat the people in our lives (including ourselves), how He calls us to do that is custom-made to each of us and the lives He created for us to live.

Since we will be using the imagery of our lives as a container garden throughout the book, think of it like this:

no two container gardens ever look the same. There may be similar characteristics, but they are never identical. So too are the lives we are meant to lead. There may be similar characteristics (like marriage, or number of children, or occupations) but no two lives will be lived identically.

The process of learning to receive God's peace in the midst of chaos is lifelong and grace-filled. While we can be assured of having access to God's perfect peace, we will not live it out perfectly. In fact, breaking up with perfect is a good thing to consider. God does not expect us to be perfect and loves us in the middle of all our messes. He did not send us Jesus to embrace those who were "perfect"' but instead to redeem and restore all of us who aren't. In Him, we are made perfect and that doesn't change if we are living "imperfectly."

As you read through this book, it is my hope that you will consider what I have said, but that you will always follow where Jesus leads you. God has a plan for your life that you do not have to make happen. The only thing He asks is that we trust Him and His plan and watch while He brings us through the chaos we will inevitably experience.

This book is divided into two parts. **Part I is all about you.** Each chapter tells a different part of the story of how important you are to God. It is important to know who you are and how much you are loved today, *without having to make everything right first*. Cultivating Peace in any of our relationships begins with allowing God to cultivate it in *us* first.

Part 2 is all about others. Each chapter focuses on allowing God to guide and direct us in His vision for us in all the relationships we may have in our life. I have included all the majors: Marriage, Children, Family, Home and Work.

I also believe in practical application. I have created a special, free, down-loadable and printable resource called Digging Deeper. Much of what I learned, I have learned through reflection, study, and trial and error. In Digging Deeper I offer reflective questions for each chapter, mini-devotions, and the tools I use to visually pay attention to why I feel more chaos than peace when the whirlwinds of life start swirling all around me. You can get it right now by visiting StephanieHaynes.net, and clicking Digging Deeper under the Cultivating Peace tab.

> *I ask God to strengthen you by his Spirit—not a brute strength but a glorious inner strength—that Christ will live in you as you open the door and invite him in. And I ask Him that with both feet planted firmly on love, you'll be able to take in with all the followers of Jesus the extravagant dimensions of Christ's love. God can do anything... far more than you could imagine or guess or request in your wildest dreams! He does it not by pushing us around but by working within us, his Spirit deeply and gently within us."*

(Ephesians 3:14-21 the Message.)

Thank you for picking up this book.

Stephanie

Part One
Laying a Good Foundation

"Yet to all who did receive him, to those who believed in his name, he gave the right to become children of God—children born not of natural descent, nor of human decision or a husband's will, but born of God. The Word became flesh and made his dwelling among us. We have seen his glory, the glory of the one and only Son, who came from the Father, full of grace and truth... Out of his fullness we have all received grace in place of grace already given. For the law was given through Moses; grace and truth came through Jesus Christ. No one has ever seen God, but the one and only Son, who is himself God and is in closest relationship with the Father, has made him known."

John 1:12-14, 15-18 NLT

Chapter One
Religion vs. Relationship

"Remain in me, and I will remain in you.
For a branch cannot produce fruit if it is
severed from the vine, and you cannot
be fruitful unless you remain in me."

John 15:4 NLT

One

At my life's most chaotic point, relationships were hardly a priority. What mattered most was doing--making sure the house was spotless, being sure to do everything required of me at work, and keeping the family calendar perfectly organized. My days were spent running from one thing on my to-do list to another. I seldom considered how my actions were affecting those around me because my worth was found in "do-ty," not in a relationship.

As I mentioned in the introduction, to represent this season God gave me the image that my life resembled an overgrown, half-dead and full-of-weeds garden container in the middle of summer that hadn't been watered or fertilized in months. At its very base was a legalistic foundation based on earning my own way through life. That foundation was the source of my chaos. At its center was the belief that I was in control and needed to remain in control if everything was to turn out the way I expected it to. The result was a huge mess of a life focused on making sure I was always doing everything "right."

Once I became a Christian, I approached living out my new-found faith in much the same way; "do-ing" for God. In retrospect, I didn't really know how to live out my faith any differently than I had been living out my life. My foundation before Jesus had been rooted in doing enough to be accepted and so, without really giving it much thought, I carried that belief with me into my new life. The result was the development of a fear that somehow God would cut me off if I wasn't good enough at following all the rules.

This is what *religion* is all about. The foundation of religion, at its center, has a belief that we are responsible for making sure our life turns out "right." This legalistic, rule-following approach to living a life of faith often leaves us just as stressed out as we were before, only now we believe there is much more at stake if we mess up so we often push ourselves even harder.

This is not what God intends: *"Remain in me, and I will remain in you. For a branch cannot produce fruit if it is severed from the vine, and you cannot be fruitful unless you remain in me."* (John 15:4 NLT)

In John chapter 15 verses 1-17, Jesus uses the illustration of a vine to show the disciples how to receive what they will need in order to live the lives He came to offer them. To remain (or abide) in Jesus means "to live, continue, or remain; to live in Him or remain in Him."[2] We remain in Jesus when we seek to learn from Him and His ways; when we depend on Him to show us what we should do. *To be fruitful*[3] means to be the recipient of what we will need in order to live fully the unique life for which we were created. If you cut off a branch of the vine, it cannot produce anything on its own. When it remains connected to the main vine, it is given the ability to do what it was created to do. The same is true for us. When our foundation is the true Vine, Jesus, we receive what's needed to do what we are called to do in a day, season, and lifetime.

This is the difference between religion and relationship. *Religion* says we have to do it all on our own. *Relationship* says we can rest in the One who can do it *for* us and *through* us. This paradigm shift allows for a new foundation to be built not on control or fear of leagalism, but upon the truth that connected to God nothing is impossible for us.

> "Choosing to develop an ongoing relationship with Jesus Christ gives us a new foundation to remain in Him one step at a time."

Having a relationship with Jesus as our foundation (referred after as a foundational relationship), means we are given *everything we need* to live the life we are called to live. When we experience a struggle and allow God to work in us and through us as we face it, we receive all we need to enable us to handle, with God's strength, whatever comes our way. This is the only foundation that can sustain us through our lives in such a way that will grant us the peace we long for in our very cores. I'm not talking about an absence of chaos, but the development of a mental state characterized by a complete trust in the plan of God, regardless of how overwhelming the circumstances may be. The presence of peace is not the absence of encountering stress or weariness, but what we receive when we turn to Jesus in those moments.

When we get stuck, when our marriages are in trouble, when we face struggles as a parent, when our homes are crazy, Jesus will show us how to follow God's will and walk through the trial with peace in our hearts not because we are in control, but because we trust the One who is. Choosing to develop an ongoing *relationship* with Jesus Christ gives us a new foundation to remain in Him one step at a time.

Developing a relationship with Jesus takes time, just like developing a relationship with a human being does. All too often though we determine that we don't have enough time to develop this relationship because there is so much we have to do. When we choose to allow Jesus to rebuild the foundation of our lives upon Him, however, we receive the time and energy to do whatever He has planned for us with love, peace, and grace. This relationship, our foundation, becomes the vine of sustenance for every other relationship in our lives.

A Jesus-centered foundation is built upon four key principles of relationships: *Submission, Respect, Forgiveness,* and *Intimacy.*

Submission refers to the act of choosing to yield or surrender to the will or authority of another out of love and respect for that authority rather than out of fear. The word "submission" used to leave a bitter taste in my mouth: "Why on earth would I ever let anyone else be 'in charge' of me?" was my response. The more I assumed responsibility for, the more overwhelmed I got. I am a strong, confident, driven woman, but *I have realized that I don't know anything compared to the knowledge of God.* The way my life started falling all to pieces is direct evidence of that. In this context, submission becomes a form of protection, rather than a limitation.

Submission to Jesus means we choose to follow His direction in living out the life God created us to live. I am free to do whatever I choose because of grace, but when I choose to live *my* life according to *my* own terms the feelings of chaos come and my life begins to overwhelm me. When I choose, because of grace, to submit to God's plan for my life I receive more peace to face what comes my way.

After submission comes *respect*. To respect Jesus means to place value on who He is. Jesus is God's Son who has been with God since the beginning.[4] He came to earth to teach us the ways of God so that we could enter into a relationship with Him and receive His forgiveness, blessing, mercy and grace.[5] In God's eyes, each of us was uniquely created for His purpose. None of us is better or worse than the other; He loves us all equally. We do not have to earn respect from God; earning is part of *religion*. To choose to not only follow where Jesus leads (submission) but also value *who* He is cultivates respect. Therefore, the very act of choosing to cultivate this foundation of a *relationship* with Jesus is a sign of respect

Forgiveness, in the context of a relationship with Jesus, is about receiving. We were born into sin.[6] God, however, is holy. He cannot connect to us then because of our sinfulness. As a result, we have lived a life apart from God. God knows this and longs to have a relationship with us, which is why He sent Jesus to not only tell us how much God loved us but to also die on a cross for us.

When Jesus died, he took all our sins with him. Every. Single. One. When Jesus was resurrected by God the door was opened for each one of us to be resurrected from our dead life in sin with Him. Because of Jesus we can be restored to a right relationship with God through forgiveness of every sin we ever commit. When we choose to believe this truth we receive Jesus as our Savior (the Redeemer of our sins and the Saver of our souls) and receive the *forgiveness* of all our past sin as well as all our present and future sin. Cultivating a foundational relationship with Jesus is to receive forgiveness and begin a new life: *"This means that anyone who belongs to Christ has become a new person. The old life is gone; a new life has begun!"* (2 Corinthians 5:17 NLT)

The final key principle of our foundational relationship is *intimacy*. There are two types of intimacy: emotional intimacy and physical intimacy. Emotional intimacy is characterized by a deep emotional connection with another person along with the presence of trust and the safety to be vulnerable. Physical intimacy involves many, if not all, of the components of emotional intimacy as well as a physical closeness (such as between a husband and wife).

Intimacy is important in any relationship, but when we choose to develop a foundational relationship with Jesus we experience it in its purest form. When we choose to move towards God through choosing to allow Jesus to lead us (submission), choosing to value Jesus for who He is and what He did for us (respect), and receive the new life given to us through Jesus' death and resurrection (forgiveness), the closer we *are drawn to* Him through God's Spirit.

The Holy Spirit is the very essence of God. He is our counselor, our teacher, and the One who reminds us of the Truth of God.[7] God sends Him to us as a deposit guaranteeing a place in heaven *for us* the moment we choose to receive forgiveness for our sins through salvation in Jesus.[8] As believers in Jesus Christ, these three; God the Father, God the Son (Jesus Christ) and God the Spirit (Holy Spirit) are One (often called The Trinity or the Holy Trinity) in our lives. We are drawn closer to the entire Trinity through this process of submission, respect and forgiveness, therefore experiencing intimacy in its purest form.

The main product of our foundational relationship with Jesus is love: we are enabled to receive a love so powerful that it transforms us from what we once were, into who we were authentically meant to be, without guilt or shame. Jesus loves us unconditionally. He accepts who we are, faults, flaws, weaknesses, and all. There is no fear of condemnation from Him.[9] He also loves us so much that He doesn't let us remain as we once were. *He* works to help us change, grow, and reach our maturity in the purpose for which we were created. When the very foundation of who we are is built upon a relationship with Jesus everything is affected.

Additionally, as we continue to choose to develop a foundational relationship with Jesus Christ, peace begins to grow. When we choose to submit, we begin the life-long process of letting go of trying to be in control of everything. This grants us an ever-deepening source of peace as we learn to relax and trust Jesus to be in charge. When we choose to respect Jesus for who He is and what He did for us, we receive the ability to begin the life-long process of ending our quest of having to do it all in order to earn our place. The more we stop trying to earn our value, the more peace we receive about the value of who we already are.

When we choose to receive forgiveness, we begin the life-long process of living as a new creation transformed by the renewing of our minds.[10] Forgiveness opens the door for Jesus to heal us, and as our hurts are healed, we receive peace about each situation that caused the hurt. When we choose to build intimacy we begin the life-long process of opening ourselves up to trust Jesus more and more. As we do this He releases us from the bondage of fear, worry, and false expectations and instead generates peace in who we are and what's going on in our lives.

Notice that I say this is a "life-long process" repeatedly. A foundational relationship with Jesus is not something we can manufacture and move on from, that's *religion*. Religion tells us to live by rules and we will be safe. It implies there is a "right way" and a "wrong way;" a perfect standard to achieve. In *relationship* there is no perfection. There is One way for all of us to draw near to God the Father; through a relationship with Jesus Christ, but how this plays out in each of our lives is unique to each one of us.[11] There is no "right way" to be a believer in Jesus Christ, but it is a process that takes a lifetime to experience. Cultivating Peace then is the life-long process we enter into once we choose to develop a foundational relationship with Jesus.

If you are feeling curious or have a desire to build a relationship with Jesus, I encourage you to pick up a Bible and read the story of Jesus in any one of the first four books of the New Testament: Matthew, Mark, Luke, or John (also called the Gospels). If you do not have a Bible, you can instead utilize Bible reference sites such as biblegateway.com.

I personally have found the peace I need in the midst of the chaos of my life because of my faith in the truth of Jesus. I have accepted that I cannot do life on my own terms and conditions well enough for long enough to create the peace I have found in Jesus. If you would like the *"peace that surpasses all comprehension"* (Philippians 4:7 NASB) to begin to permeate in your life as well and begin a foundational relationship with Jesus, I invite you to open your heart and invite Jesus in. I know that sounds a bit odd but think of it like this: inviting Jesus into your heart is like inviting a friend into your home; you ask them over, invite them in, and begin a conversation. Any words telling Jesus that you realize you are a sinner, that you believe Jesus is who He says He is, and that you would like forgiveness so you have access to the peace God offers through a relationship with His Son will do. God knows you, and He will listen to your heart when words may not come easily. If you are unsure of what to say, you can speak the following prayer:

Jesus? I want to know Your peace. I want to know You. I am tired, overwhelmed, and need help. I believe You are who You say You are—God's Son, born of a virgin, who lived a sinless life before dying on the cross for my sins and that You were raised from the dead so that in You I might have a new life. I have been a sinner and I want to be forgiven so I can begin a new life with You as my foundation. Please forgive me. Amen.

If you have been in relationship with Jesus, but have come to realize that maybe you want to reestablish that relationship as the foundation of your life, here is a prayer especially for you:

Jesus, I know You and love You, but I do not feel as much peace as I believe I could have from a relationship with You. Please help me to draw near to You. Please bring to mind any sin in my life so I may repent of it. If there is something in my life that is keeping me from fully devoting myself to You, please help me let it go. I choose again to ask you to be the Savior of my life. Please guide me. Amen.

Take a moment before continuing on to really let your

decision sink in. New believer or long time believer, you are a child of God, sister to Christ himself! You are forgiven of EVERYTHING, no matter how awful you think it is. You are pure and holy in the sight of God who sees Jesus' sinless life in place of yours. Hallelujah! Please don't keep this decision to yourself like I did! Share your decision with a pastor or Christian friend or family member as soon as possible!

• • •

Developing a relationship takes building trust, one step at a time. Whether you have begun to build a foundational relationship with Jesus for the first time ever, or have had Him as your foundation for a while now, I would like to share a few practical suggestions for nourishing that relationship. Cultivating peace is an imperfect process; sometimes we will feel peace in all the chaos of our lives and other times it can feel like the chaos takes over and makes a mess of things. Having something to "do" that opens us up to the peace Jesus is offering no matter the situation can give us the strength to choose His peace over trying to fix everything on our own.

1. **Talk to others about Jesus.** When we seek out fellow believers and ask questions, share what we are learning, and voice our fears and doubts, Jesus will be there with us to guide us. Jesus himself says, *"For where two or three gather in my name, there am I with them."* (Matthew 18:20)

2. **Read about Jesus in the Bible.** Reading the Gospels (Matthew, Mark, Luke, and John) is an excellent place to start.

3. **Think about how Jesus treated those around Him.** When we stop to think about how Jesus responds to the people in His life, we gain a better understanding of who He is.

4. **Memorize things Jesus says that are meaningful to you.** Jesus knew that Scripture was the way to defeat the temptations He suffered (Matthew 4:1-11). Reciting scripture can help us in times of temptation, stress, and fear and can keep us focused on God over the lies of the world.

5. **"Talk" to Jesus.** Pray. If you "get lost in your mind" as you pray, consider journaling your thoughts, questions, longings, and fears.

Religion will keep you stuck in the chaos;

Relationship will set you on the path of peace.

Let's Pray

Father God, Thank you for desiring to build a relationship with us! Please help us to let go of performance-based religion. Give us the wisdom we need to live in the freedom of Your grace as we learn to build a relationship with You through your Son Jesus. Amen!

"...now we are free to live in the Spirit and to be truly right with God. As free people, the Spirit gives us the characteristics of Jesus; we, too, can freely love in joy and peace. We can have patience along with kindness and faithfulness that can only come from the Father. We can reflect the goodness of God while being gentle in operating with self-control. For those who follow Him (Jesus) and live in the Spirit, these characteristics or fruits are a gift from God. As we grow in the faith we find that we belong to God and can walk daily in the Spirit."

(Galatians 5:22-23, the Voice)

Chapter Two
Who God Says You Are

"I know how to live on almost nothing or
with everything. I have learned the secret of
living in every situation, whether it is with a
full stomach or empty, with plenty or little.
For I can do everything through Christ,
who gives me strength."

Philippians 4:12-13 NLT

Two

When you were younger, what did you dream your life would be like? Did you dream of being a corporate executive? A chef? A world traveler? A wife and mother? When I was growing up, I envisioned my future adult life as a teacher. From a very early age (second grade to be precise) I knew I wanted to teach. Maybe it was from watching Laura Ingalls on *Little House on the Prairie*. Or maybe it was my second-grade teacher, Mrs. Brennan, who taught me how to make my own peanut butter which I thought was the coolest thing ever. Whatever the reason was, teaching became what I wanted to do most. I even played school with my little sister and made up pretend lessons for an invisible class.

I spent ten years as a high school English teacher and loved (almost) every minute of it. Everything I did revolved around "my kids" and their education and activities. The majority of my "free summers" meant working a second job and planning out my entire school year down to the homework assignments I would give and when. Hours were given to coaching the cheerleaders, organizing the Renaissance committee rallies, attending plays and sporting events, and running the English department.[12] The last five years of my career I was part of a team of teachers dedicated to improving the educational success of our most at-risk students through preparing them for a career in the health industry.[13] I loved that part of my career as a teacher the best. Our class size was very small (20 student maximum) so we got to know all of them on a deeply personal level. We got to pour into them and, as a result, they gave us their best, often at a level they didn't know they had. It was extremely rewarding to watch them risk and try and succeed beyond anything they ever thought possible. The more I poured into them, the more they responded, and the more value I thought I had.

When we moved to South Carolina, I had to leave all of that behind. Additionally, my husband asked me to stay at home permanently since his new position would provide financially for me to do so and require more traveling from him. I had never in all my wildest dreams ever considered being a stay-at-home mom; that felt like a step *backward* on my journey. However, I was exhausted and overwhelmed. Obtaining a new state credential meant filing forms and finding a job right away (which I was unprepared to do) and so I agreed to stay home. It wasn't a joyous relief. Instead, it felt like the death of my identity: I had worked so hard to become a teacher that I didn't know who I would be if I wasn't one.

For the next several years it seemed as if my dream of ever teaching again was dead; there was just no way for me to go back. Feeling trapped, but wanting to succeed, I spent many years trying to create a new identity as a stay-at-home mom. Honestly, it felt as if that title meant I no longer had any identity at all. I longed to be important somehow. To make a difference. To *be* somebody, and all I got to do all day every day involved laundry, diapers, shopping, and cleaning up. At the time, I believed that I needed to "do" in order to have value and being a stay-at-home mom didn't seem to be really *doing* anything. I tried to fill that need for a new identity by serving: whether it was at my daughters school or in the children's and women's ministries at church, but all that did was increase the level of chaos in my life.

I had had a dream all my life of being a teacher. Without that dream to guide me I had no idea who I was which led me to strive for value everywhere else. I am sure you have dreams too. What happens when that dream ends? What happens if those dreams are never fulfilled? What happens when that dream dies and where we find ourselves does not fit in with our hopes or expectations?

The act of cultivating peace begins with a foundational relationship with Jesus Christ, but the strength of that foundation is adversely affected if we don't know who God says we are. My value was in what I did, and when I felt I was doing nothing I believed I had no value, which caused me to strive harder to create one. Even though I had a new foundational relationship with Jesus, I still believed I had to earn my value with him; I believed I had to prove I was worth dying for.

What about you? Honestly, do you believe who God says you are? Do you know what you mean to him? Those deep longings of our hearts are evidence of God's love *for* us. He wants to draw us closer to Him, so He instills longings into our hearts to help us turn to Him.[14] Unfortunately, because of the culture we live in, we often turn everywhere else but Him for our fulfillment. We strive harder to achieve, to change, to earn; all in the hopes that we will become *enough*. What happens if you just stop *doing*, though? Will you be enough?

The truth is God loves you. Right. This. Moment. He has loved you with an everlasting love.[15] A love that is not dependent upon what you do or don't do. He loves you simply because He does. You cannot earn a greater amount of His love than you already possess by doing more and, because of Jesus, you can never be separated from it.[16]

The peace we receive in a foundational relationship with Jesus can best permeate our very souls when we accept who God says we are:

We are unconditionally loved, *right now.* *"And may you have the power to understand, as all God's people should, how wide, how long, how high, and how deep his love is. May you experience the love of Christ, though it is too great to understand fully. Then you will be made complete with all the fullness of life and power that comes from God."* Ephesians 3:17-19 NLT

We are fearfully and wonderfully made, *right now.* *"I praise you because I am fearfully and wonderfully made; your works are wonderful, I know that full well."* Psalm 139:14 NIV

We are redeemed from all our sin, *right now.* *"For you know that it was not with perishable things such as silver or gold that you were redeemed from the empty way of life handed down to you from your ancestors, but with the precious blood of Christ, a lamb without blemish or defect."* 1 Peter 1:18-19 NIV

Learning to accept who God says we are is the most freeing, peace-instilling thing we can do. My history includes a deep struggle against feeling worthless. As a result, I was always searching for something to make me feel worthy--a specific jeans size, a number on a scale, a promotion at work, a certain amount of money in the bank. This search was endless: I would achieve one thing, only to have the "high" of success wear off, and so the search would start again. Or, I would fulfill a longing and then lose it (say in reaching a number on the scale and then gaining weight), which caused me to berate myself for being a loser. I was a mess of discontent.

Why do I share all this with you? Because I want you to understand how important it is to get to know yourself, to actually learn to delight in who God made you to be right now whether or not those longings in your heart are ever fulfilled. Those dreams you have, the longings within your heart, are important. Much more important, though, is first learning to love who you are without those longings fulfilled.

> "Learning to accept who God says we are is the most freeing, peace-instilling thing we can do."

When my struggle to accept the truth of who God says I am was at its climax, a friend reminded me that in God's eyes I was already His *beloved*. He sent His Son to die for me. ME--a woman who couldn't even look at herself in the mirror without seeing ugliness. ME--a woman who feared her every move was being scrutinized and feared equally she was being overlooked. ME--a woman who believed she had messed everything up. **I had accepted the free gift of salvation, but I still didn't believe I was worthy of it.**

In God's eyes, you and I are amazing. So amazing in fact that He sent His son to die for us so He could draw each of us closer to himself. Yes, this includes YOU, the woman who believes she's messed everything up. YOU, the woman who believes she has way too many sins in her life. YOU, the woman who believes she is a lost cause. YOU, the woman who desperately longs to have value and believes she has to do in order to earn it.

You are amazing to God right this moment. Period.

Let that sink in a while before continuing…

Earlier in this book I shared how God imprinted the vision of my life being like an over-grown, half-dead, full-of-weeds garden planter that hadn't been watered or fertilized in months. I also shared how He began "re-potting" my life. The first step was to replace my legalistic, control-based foundation with a relationship with Jesus Christ. The next part, as in gardening, is filling that container with nourishing soil. Think of it like this. If the life we have been given is represented by a container used to plant flowers, and the rock-based foundation for healthy plants is represented by our relationship with Jesus Christ, then our personal nourishment comes from the "soil" of God's Word. Our soil doesn't have to be your run-of-the-mill soil. It becomes a nutrient-rich "super soil" when we choose to *trust* God at His word.

The first cup of our new "super soil" is to choose to *believe* that who God says we are at this moment is worthy of being loved. In order to receive His peace about who He says we are we need to understand *why* it is so hard for us to believe we are loved by God in the first place. It is one thing to be told to love who you are. It is a whole other thing to actually *believe* you are loved. When we believe we are not worthy of love it can cause us to do all sorts of things in an effort to earn it. God's love for us is the same today as it was when we were little girls and will remain constant until we meet Him face-to-face.

When we choose to *believe* we are loved right NOW, to accept the truth that God won't love us more when we get our act together, and that He doesn't love us less when we don't, we can enter into a change in perspective. The fears and worries that keep us on the treadmill of "do-ty" in order to earn that love can begin to lose their power and be replaced with the strength to choose to believe God at his Word.

> "The ability to believe who God says we are comes in developing a relationship with ourselves and learning the truth of who we really are."

When we begin to believe that truth we are given the ability to receive the peace we long for.

For a long time, I didn't believe I was worthy of love. I believed it was something I had to earn; if I could behave in just the right way, do all the right things, and present myself in just the right way then I would be worthy. It seemed completely foreign to accept I was loved just for being *me* and that nothing I could do could make God love me more *or* less. Why was that? I believe it's rooted in acceptance. The world (and sometimes the people in my life) didn't accept me as I was so I believed I was unworthy. This false belief caused me to always "do" to the detriment of my own health and well-being. From the moment I woke up, to the moment I fell into bed, I was either taking care of everyone else or taking care to be sure I was living up to some impossible standard. I was actually choosing to participate in the chaos because I believed making everyone else happy was the way to find peace: if I did enough to be loved I could then relax... only I could never achieve enough and peace never came.

I wonder if it's the same for you. Have you been beaten down by trying to keep up with unrealistic expectations and have come to believe you are unworthy of love because those expectations can never be satisfied? The good news is that we can choose to stop that sort of thinking. We can choose to stop believing we are unworthy, stop believing we must "do" to be loved, and stop engaging in behaviors that are detrimental to our health. The ability to believe who God says we are comes in developing a relationship with ourselves and learning the truth of who we really are.

Our foundational relationship with Jesus Christ gives us the appropriate framework for all the other relationships in our life, including building a relationship with ourselves. It may seem silly to create a relationship with yourself, but I am certain of this: when we know who and whose we are we are able to love ourselves. When we know how to love ourselves, we can much more effectively love those God brings into our lives. When we talked about developing a relationship with Jesus I shared with you four key principles of relationships: **Submission, Respect, Forgiveness,** and **Intimacy.** Those same factors are very important to your relationship with yourself.

As with building our relationship with Jesus, our first step in building a relationship with ourselves is *submission*. In order to create a lasting, peace-centered relationship with ourselves we need to accept that we cannot (nor should we) be in control of our lives. When we let go of trying to be in control,

God can come in, removing the weariness that comes from trying to figure it all out. When we choose to submit to God, we can let go of the weight of being responsible for everything in our life. As we do that we learn we can trust that God is capable *and* will show us our part in anything He wants us to do.

Submission, then, is God's gift to us, to protect us against weariness, and the inevitable feelings of chaos that come from shouldering the weight of our life on our own. When we submit, releasing the burden of having to figure everything out on our own, we are freed to discover what He is doing in our lives. As a result, we can come to understand we are loved, cared for, and blessed. When we learn that, our relationship with ourselves blossoms because we are free to discover who we are instead of trying to figure out who we are supposed to be.

For example, instead of trying to make everything happen according to how I thought it was supposed to happen, I began to ask God what He wanted to happen. It wasn't easy. I was afraid something might happen that would make me look bad. As I began to listen to the whispers of the Holy Spirit, however, I would find that at the end of the day no one complained I had not lived up to the expectations I had been living with *in my head*. Instead, I began to actually enjoy my kids and my husband and they began to express more love for me. Shopping got done. Cleaning got done, but the biggest changes happened within myself: I realized that I was free to just be and that God would make sure what I thought I needed to get done in my own strength got done without my having to make sure it did. The feelings of chaos I had been living with for years slowly bagan to fade.

This is a life-long process. Sometimes I am able to submit cheerfully and without fear. Other times I find myself all stressed-out and caught up in taking control again. However, because of God's grace, we are able to receive His forgiveness and mercy as we learn how to trust Him more completely. Here are a few suggestions to help you begin this part of the process:

1. Ask God to remind you when you are trying to be in control of things in your life.

2. Share your struggle with a trusted friend who will hold you accountable to letting God be in control of the decisions you face.

3. Offer one thing at a time to God in which He can lead you. It's okay to take the time to develop trust in God. He is patient and will wait for you.

4. Thank God when He leads you through a period of struggling for the purpose of learning to trust Him.

5. Seek to cultivate a contented heart, appreciating what you have and who you are right now, and give God praise for it all.

Second in this process is learning to *respect* yourself. Respecting ourselves is one of the most important things we can ever do in cultivating peace. When we do not respect ourselves we allow others to walk all over us, make choices for us, and involve us in things that further degrade our opinion of ourselves; all things that steal our peace. I remember being willing to do whatever it took to be liked by boys who I wanted to like me. I remember wanting to be accepted by the popular crowd and sacrificing what I knew to be the right thing to do in order to fit in. Why? I didn't respect myself.

Respect often seems difficult doesn't it? If you are struggling to like who you are, especially if your plan for your life isn't the same as the reality you are currently living, then respect can seem like a joke. Who can respect someone who doesn't live up to expectations? But this is not what Biblical respect entails. Respecting ourselves doesn't mean comparing ourselves to those around us, or even comparing ourselves to the success of our own plans. It means we don't think of ourselves as less than anyone around us, period. The Bible puts it like this:

"The only accurate way to understand ourselves is by what God is and by what he does for us, not by what we are and what we do for him. In this way, we are like the various parts of a human body. Each part gets its meaning from the body as a whole, not the other way around. The body we're talking about is Christ's body of chosen people. Each of us finds our meaning and function as a part of his body. But as a chopped-off finger or cut-off toe we wouldn't amount to much, would we? So since we find ourselves fashioned into all these excellently formed and marvelously functioning parts in Christ's body, let's just go ahead and be what we were made to be, without enviously or pridefully comparing ourselves with each other, or trying to be something we aren't." (Romans 12:4-6, The Message Bible)

To respect ourselves is to accept that we are not like anyone else around us without fearing that we are not good enough. When we allow this truth to sink into our parched souls and *believe it is true*, our relationship with ourselves further deepens into accepting who we are with all our strengths and weaknesses. God says you are essential to His master plan for the whole wide world, past, present and future. He designed you for a specific, integral part. That's the truth of who God says you are. Believing that truth breaks down the false belief that we are not enough unless we do or achieve or succeed.

For the longest time, I believed I was not good enough and that thought process caused all kinds of chaos within my thought life which directly affected my actions. Since I didn't respect who I was, because who I *thought I was* didn't fit with the idea of who I *thought I was supposed to be*, I was constantly inconsistent in my behaviors and reactions. I was always trying to be whoever the person in front of me needed to be. That led to all kinds of chaos: I needed to constantly change to be who I thought my kids wanted or who I thought my husband wanted or who I thought my friends wanted. The truth is that they loved me for me, but I couldn't believe that. Little by little, though, God is eroding away that fear and replacing it with the ability to respect who He made me to be, in each season I am living in. He wants to do this for you too.

Learning to respect ourselves doesn't always come easily. While I still struggle in this area, here are a few things that have worked for me:

1. Invite God to share His vision of who you are to Him and choose to believe what He shows you.

2. Read and meditate on the Serenity Prayer.[17]

3. Try something new. When you face a challenge, and get through it, there's a sense of accomplishment that grants us respect for ourselves.

4. Treat yourself as well as you treat those around you. When you respect yourself, you make sure your needs are met just as much as you work to meet other's needs.

5. Help others learn to respect themselves too. When I listen to other's struggles it reminds me that everyone, no matter who they are or their station in life, struggles with something. When I accept this, I offer myself respect.

The third key principle of building a relationship with ourselves in order to believe who God says we are involves learning to receive the forgiveness we have been given. When we accept the free gift of salvation from God through Jesus Christ, we are forgiven of all our sins, no matter how big we think they are. We. Are. CLEAN! It is one thing to know that, though, and another to feel it so deeply in our hearts that we can live like it, isn't it?

Every time I make a mistake, mess up, hurt someone (even unintentionally), or sin in my angry reactions, I feel absolutely terrible. I say I am sorry. I ask for forgiveness from God and those who may have been involved (when appropriate), but there is always one person standing in judgment, condemning me. Myself. Yep, the hardest person to forgive is ME. I can say to anyone out there that forgiveness should be given freely. We all make mistakes. I can quotes scripture on it too. Yet, when it comes to receiving God's forgiveness myself, I absolutely dig my heels in like a stubborn mule who doesn't want to move. I refuse to let it go. Why is that?

I believe it has a lot to do with expectations. I have HUGE expectations for myself and when I make any kind of mistake, I let myself down. Anyone else around me could make the same mistake hundreds of times, and I can forgive them for it. But me? I make a mistake once and I am unforgivable.

We are no less than anyone around us; we are special in our own right and have been hand-crafted for a special purpose in God's master plan. Fulfilling that purpose, however, is not going to be easy. We will make mistakes. We will take wrong turns and try out shortcuts. Therefore, it's time to learn how to receive forgiveness for ourselves.

While I will be the first to admit that receiving forgiveness is not something I do well (and I am working on that), I do understand its importance. When I hold on to mistakes I have made in the past, I tend to become stagnant; I don't know how to move forward with this mistake hanging over me so I just don't. It's like I am on one of those little kiddie rides at an amusement park. You know the ones that usually have little boats or motorcycles and just go around and around and around? It is like I am on one of those and I cannot get off. When that happens I cannot move forward on the path God has set before me. I try, but all I do is come back to where I messed up. The longer I go without believing I have been forgiven, the more fear creeps in and steals my hope that I will ever be free. It works like a shackle that holds me rooted to the spot where the mistake happened. I try to break free in my own strength, but I get frustrated, overwhelmed, and worn out.

This is what happens when fear, not love, begins to rule our hearts: fear of not being good enough, fear of making another mistake, fear of not meeting our own expectations so we don't even try. Out of love Jesus came and died on the cross for our sins to be forgiven so that we *may have life and have it to the full."* (John 10:10) You are a woman, like me, who has probably made many mistakes in her life. Guess what? Once you enter into a relationship with Jesus Christ, you are forgiven of Every. Single. One. Of. Them! Your expectations for yourself do not need to be greater than God's. He expected that you would make many mistakes; that's why He sent His Son ahead of time to forgive you for them before you even committed any of them.

Some of the biggest blockers to accepting who God says you are right now are hidden wounds that have not healed because you have not allowed the truth of His forgiveness to become real for you. There is no mistake, no sin you may have committed, that is too big for God's forgiveness. While you may be suffering the consequences from those times, none is too much to bear with God's grace. Put your armor on,[18] stand and face your mistakes, and watch the blood of Jesus cover them all. That is how to break free of the chains that have shackled you to your past and kept you unable to find peace in today.

Like I have said before, I am still working on this issue too, but here are a few things I have found that help me learn to receive the forgiveness I have already been given:

1. Confront your past. You cannot forgive without admitting you are a fallible sinner. Get real with God and let it all out.

2. Look for strengths that were developed from experiencing the consequences of your mistakes. Are you wiser, stronger, more compassionate?

3. Phrase your issue as if you were talking to a friend. What advice would you give to her?

4. Share your experience with others. Not only can you help others possibly avoid making the same mistake, but you also will receive confirmation that you are normal. We are ALL sinners.

5. Examine your expectations of yourself. Are you holding yourself to a higher standard than you hold those around you? Why?

You'd think that *intimacy*, the fourth principle of a healthy relationship with ourselves, would come naturally wouldn't you? I mean, we are with ourselves all day long so aren't we close enough? Not really. I have found that while I can easily get to know someone else, getting to know myself is, well... difficult. I can't really talk to myself (well, I do actually, but I keep that a secret!) and doing things by myself is uncomfortable. Sometimes, too, I think it's much easier to hide away my own desires. I mean, we aren't supposed to only talk about what we want, right? So in order to avoid social sabotage it just seems easier to go along with those around me, being careful to not make waves, letting other's opinions become my own for the sake of getting along. I wonder if it's the same for you.

I have found, however, that it is not easier.

When we don't know who we are in Christ, we are vulnerable to influences that steer us off the path that God created for us. We each were created as a unique individual with strengths, weaknesses, desires, and experiences that make us who we are and qualify us to fulfill the purpose for which we were created.

"If we don't take the time to discover ourselves, we run the risk of trying to be like someone else, therefore missing out on the amazing person we are."

If we don't take the time to discover ourselves, we run the risk of trying to be like someone else, therefore missing out on the amazing person we are. We may even fall into sinful behaviors, destructive relationships, or other painful experiences, further maneuvering us away from who we were meant to be and the life we were meant to live.

In addition to being able to stick close to God's plan for our lives, getting to know ourselves also helps us become a positive influence on those around us. Think about it. If you know who you are, chances are you will like yourself much better than if you don't. When you like yourself, you exude confidence. Confidence is a big part of influence. When we lack self-confidence, we look to others to give it to us. When we have confidence in ourselves, we can be the influence instead.

What does the Bible have to say about all this? One of my favorite verses in reminding me to be who God created me to be is Romans 12:2. *"Do not conform any longer to the pattern of this world, but be transformed by the renewing of your mind. Then you will be able to test and approve what God's will is— his good, pleasing and perfect will."* I am in a process of having my mind renewed continually. (The verb "renewing" is written in the present progressive, implying a continuing pattern.) I know I am not perfect and that I will make mistakes. However, the process I undergo when I remember to come back to God and His plan helps me to learn about who I am.

Intimacy is key in being able to accept who God says we are because it offers us the opportunity to get to know who God made us to be. It requires us to trust God, which feels like a huge risk. What if who we are doesn't meet our expectations of who we hoped to be?

I shared at the beginning of this chapter how my dream for myself was to be a high school English teacher and how much I loved being one. I also shared how devastated I as when that "identity" was removed from my daily existence. Everything *I thought I was*, was tied up in being a high school English teacher; that turned out to be a gross underestimation of the identity I have in Christ. Since the last day of my public education teaching career, I have had more opportunities to teach, but none of them were ever on my radar. I have been a homeschooling mom. I have been a children's ministry leader. I have taught my children Christ-centered values as I learn to live them out. I have taught hundreds of women how to trust God at His word and encouraged them to take huge courageous steps of faith. I do not share this with you to self-promote; only to share that often our view of ourselves is so limited compared to what God's view is. Imagine if I had spent all my time trying to be the only type of teacher *I* thought I could be; how much I would have missed out on! When we make the choice to allow God to reveal to us who He made us to be, a whole new world of possibilities opens up for us.

Discover who you are, what is important to you, and who you are without the influence of anyone else. When you choose to do this you give yourself the opportunity to receive the courage to keep the confidence that God placed in you when He created you. When we keep this confidence, when we choose not to conform because who we are is enough, we will have peace.

So, how to begin to develop intimacy? Here are a few ways that are helping me:

1. Spend time in prayer and reflection seeking out how God sees you.

2. Learn your personal love language and communicate it to others around you. The book *The Five Love Languages* by Gary Chapman is a great resource.

3. Learn your personality type and how it influences, and is influenced, by the other personality types. I have used *Personality Plus* by Florence Littauer.

4. Try new things (food, activities, trips, classes) and discover for yourself what you like and don't like.

5. Open up to the possibility that you are more than what you do in this current season of life, and that

God has plans to use your gifts and talents in a myriad of ways. Where might He be guiding you?

While intimacy is listed as the last key principle of the process of learning to accept the truth of who God says we are, it is by no means the least important. In fact, developing intimacy is a secondary benefit of all facets of working through the rest of this process. We know better who we are when we seek to understand what it means for us to submit to God as individuals, learn to respect ourselves, and receive forgiveness.

Learning to trust God at his word about who we are is only the first of many cups of nourishing super-soil available to us. He has much more in store for us.

Let's Pray

Father God, give us Your eyes so we may see ourselves as You do. Help us to believe we are Your beloved, forgiven of the sins we commit. Teach us how to love ourselves as You do. Help us to believe what You say about who we are to You. In Jesus' name, Amen.

"Those people who are listening to Me, those people who hear what I say and live according to My teachings— you are like a wise man who built his house on a rock, on a firm foundation. When storms hit, rain pounded down and waters rose, levies broke and winds beat all the walls of that house. But the house did not fall because it was built upon rock."
Matthew 7:24-25

Chapter Three

Trusting God at His Word

"Oh, the joys of those who do not follow
the advice of the wicked, or stand around
with sinners, or join in with mockers. But
they delight in the law of the Lord, meditating
on it day and night. They are like trees planted
along the riverbank, bearing fruit in each
season. Their leaves never wither, and
they prosper in all they do."

Psalm 1:1-3 NLT

Three

Do you ever believe that if only you could get the house picked up, or finish the laundry, or check off that last thing on your to-do list that *then* you'd be able to sit and enjoy those around you? Or, have you ever felt guilty about sitting down to relax when you have so many other things to do? Have you ever stopped to ask why that is? Why do we as women continually run ourselves ragged, often to the point of exhaustion, just to get up the next day and do it all again? What is the point in that? I'll tell you a secret: there is no point! It is a ploy used by the enemy to steal our peace, and boy has it worked!

While taking care of others can be a good thing, doing so to the detriment of our own health is not. When we are stressed, exhausted, and cranky it affects everyone around us, yet we work so hard at meeting everyone else's needs that there isn't enough of us left to care for ourselves. Jesus says in John 10:10 (Message): *"The thief approaches with malicious intent, looking to steal, slaughter, and destroy; I came to give life with joy and abundance."* A life spent in "busyness" taking care of everyone else around us, without making sure to take care of ourselves, is a stolen life. We--you and I and everyone around us--are meant to have a life of joy and abundance, but each of us has to make sure that happens for ourselves. No one else can do it for us.

> "A life spent in "busy-ness" taking care of everyone else around us, without making sure to take care of ourselves, is a stolen life."

I spent years taking care of everyone and everything around me to the detriment of my own health. I chose to accept as truth the lie that I could only relax after everything was done and everyone else's needs were taken care of. Only, that list was never complete; I could never finish everything or take care of everyone and still have time in the day to relax. I had come to believe that if I could just control what was going on all around me I could then relax and "be" at peace. I searched endlessly for just the right schedule or daily routine that would give me the balance I craved. I read millions of magazine articles, books, and blogs devoted to helping me organize my time so I could "have it all."

The problem though is that we were never supposed to have it all in the first place. Paul, in his first letter to the Corinthian church, says: *"Everything is permissible for me, but not everything is beneficial. Everything is permissible, but not everything is constructive."* (1 Corinthians 10:23 NIV) I was trying so hard to do it all that I continually put myself at the very bottom of the list. I had taken on more than God had asked of me and ended up drained and malnourished. That is not God's plan for me or for you either.

What I believe God wants from all of us is to choose to rely on Him to be in charge of our lives. Actually *believing* the promises contained in the Bible makes all the difference in whether or not we are able to receive God's peace in spite of the inevitable chaos that will come into our lives. That container I potted on my back porch during a burst of spring-time energy looked great when I finished, but after several months of neglect it was an overgrown, dried-out, weed-filled mess. When we spend all of our time taking care of everyone else, and leave no time to take care of ourselves, our lives can become just like that planter: over-scheduled, void of personal care and covered with lies about what we are "supposed" to do. There is no peace in that kind of life. When you are nourished you are able to nourish those relationships around you. When you are nourished you are able to be patient and focus on what's in front of you without worry or fear. When you are nourished you are able to thrive:

> *"But blessed is the one who trusts in the Lord, whose*
> *confidence is in him. They will be like a tree planted*
> *by the water that sends out its roots by the stream. It does*
> *not fear when heat comes; its leaves are always green. It has*
> *no worries in a year of droughtand never fails to bear fruit."*

Jeremiah 17:7-8 NIV

The act of cultivating peace, that mental state characterized by a complete trust in the plan of God no matter how overwhelming our circumstances may be, requires us to trust God's ways over our own ideas about how we believe things *should* be. How do we know we can trust God at His word, though?

When I first opened a Bible I was overwhelmed. It was huge for one thing. I didn't understand the terminology either; books, chapters, verses; it all was very confusing. Also, the fact that there were different versions was confusing. Sometimes someone would say a verse one way and someone else would say it differently. I remember one time looking at my Bible and trying to follow along with the pastor who was using a different version and wondering why I couldn't find what he was saying. I am not sure what the Bible means to you. It may be a treasured source of wisdom and guidance. It may be a book you have seen used and referred to but never read. Or, it may be just another book. Either way, before we can discuss trusting God at his word, we need to understand exactly what His word *is*.

The Bible (God's Word) is a love letter from God to each one of us. Not only does God love us so much that He (1) sent His Son to die for our sins in order to resurrect us into new lives in Jesus, and (2) sent His Holy Spirit to be our counselor and teacher, but He also (3) worked through others to write it all down so we could always have a way to grow in our faith. The result is the Bible.

The Bible is comprised of 66 different "books." Each book contains chapters and verses. So, when someone references a verse they name it by book, chapter, and then verse: Jeremiah 17:7-8 refers to the book of Jeremiah, chapter 17, verses 7 and 8. The original Bible was not notated by chapter and verse numbers; those were added later so we could find sections of scripture easily.

The books of the Bible are also broken up into the Old Testament (OT) and the New Testament (NT). "The word "testament" means "covenant," which is a contract or agreement between two parties. The 39 books of the Old Testament tell about the agreement between God and His chosen people the Israelites (or Hebrews or Jews). The 27 books of the

New Testament tell about the covenant (agreement, promise) between
God and the rest of humankind
through the life of Jesus and His
followers."[19] Additionally, the Bible
is also referenced through different
versions. Notations like NKJ (New
King James), NIV (New International
Version), NLT (New Living Translation), and MSG (the Message) (just
to name a few) refer to the style of
translation that is used. (There is way more to the Bible than
what I have written here. If you want to know more I highly
recommend <u>Knowing the Bible 101</u> by Bruce Bickel and
Stan Jantz.)

> "It's one thing to
> read a Bible verse.
> It's another thing
> entirely to actually
> believe what it
> says is true."

It's one thing to read a Bible verse. It's another thing
entirely to actually believe what it says is true. To simply read
it is to add a other thing to our already crowded to-do lists.
To study it, however, to savor and spend time meditating
(thinking) about what it is saying and apply it to our lives, is
how we are nourished. As the truth of scripture soaks into our
hearts, we are given strength to try and do what it says. As we
do that we are given the opportunity to see that God is faithful.

When I live my life on my own terms I create all kinds
of stress and live in a state of chaos. When I choose instead
to let God lead, I am given all I need to be able to relax,
trusting that what needs to get done will get done. When I let
God lead, He keeps me from saying yes when I should say no,
without guilt. When I choose to let God lead, I am given the
strength to keep going when life gets tough. Trusting God at

His word is our starting point to learning to receive His gift of nourishment. When we are nourished we are better able to participate with God in the life He has created for us to live.

There are many promises from the Bible that have affected my life. However, there are four in particular that have formed the "super-soil" of my life that continually nourishes me. These promises helped me to stop doing it all for everyone else and start taking care of myself. I hope they will have a positive impact on you as well.

The first (and most important) cup of anyone's "super soil" is to believe we are loved by God. (Chapter 2) The rest of our "super-soil" can come from the following four promises.

Promise One:
God's peace is available no matter what we are facing.

*"Don't worry about anything; instead, pray about everything. Tell God what you need, and thank him for all he has done. **Then you will experience God's peace, which exceeds anything we can understand.** His peace will guard your hearts and minds as you live in Christ Jesus."*
(Philippians 4:6-7 NLT)

This verse invites us into the lifelong process of turning our worries into prayers that thank God and ask Him for what we need. As we do that, His peace comes to guard us. Said another way, God's peace comes when we choose to give our worries and fears to Him instead of trying to fix everything ourselves. When we choose to lay down our worries and ask God to help us, before forming our own plan or taking things into our own hands, we let go of the weight of them. Our faith grows as we watch God take care of our worries one by one.[20] As we learn to trust in Him more deeply, He develops within us the ever-present peace we long for *no matter what chaos comes into our lives*. When we get caught up in the web of worry once again (and we will) it becomes easier to let go and receive His life-giving peace once again to carry us through.

Promise Two:
God is in control even when life seems to be chaotic.

> *"O Eternal One, I know our lives are in Your hands.*
> *It is not in us to direct our own steps—we need You.*
> *Discipline me, Eternal One, but do so fairly."*
> (Jeremiah 10:23-24 The Voice)

The second cup of "super soil" that nourishes us to be able to receive God's peace involves asking Him what we should do with the time we have been given each day. Do you realize how much time and energy we spend agonizing over decisions and trying to figure everything out? When we choose to rely on God to guide us and pay attention to how His guidance is bringing us more peace, even in the midst of chaos, our trust and reliance on Him can grow even deeper. As our trust grows deeper, we are able to see with better clarity the path marked out for us so that our focus becomes narrower. As a result, our lives become simpler. We were created with a purpose, and I believe our unrest comes because our souls long to fulfill that purpose, but the noise of the world's "should's" and "supposed to's" has clouded it. When we let God lead us, we are given the knowledge of what we can let go of so that our time and energies are saved for what we were meant to do instead of being drained away by unintended responsibilities.

Promise Three:
God will guide us through the chaos.

> *"Trust in the Lord with all your heart; do not*
> *depend on your own understanding. Seek his will*
> *in all you do, and he will show you which path to take."*
> (Proverbs 3:5-6 NLT)

The third cup of "super soil" is filled with trusting God to order the way we spend our time. How often does the state of our to-do list dictate our mood? If we complete it successfully we are jubilant. If we don't, we feel like we have failed in some way. Who exactly creates that list? Have you ever stopped to consider what God would place on that list? When we seek God's will in all we do, this verse reveals the promise that He *will* show us which path to take -- in His timing and according to His plan. From when to work versus when to rest, to how to spend our money, God knows better than we do what later today, tomorrow, next week, or even next year will hold. Therefore, isn't He much more qualified than we to determine whether or not the laundry, or whatever else is on our to-do list, gets done today? When we choose to believe this truth, and watch God take action in our lives, it can become easier to trust God's way over our own. Our lives can then become more ordered than chaotic the more we allow God to lead.

Promise Four:
God's plan eliminates the unnecessary.

> *"You say, "I am allowed to do anything"— but not*
> *everything is good for you. You say, "I am allowed to*
> *do anything"— but not everything is beneficial."*
> (1 Corinthians 10:23 NLT)

The fourth cup of "super soil" gives us the ability to know when to say "yes" and when to say "no." There is so much out there for us to choose from every day, isn't there? How can we ever know what is beneficial for us and what is not? When we choose to follow God's direction, allowing His peace to be our guide, we will be given the ability to decide (referred to as discernment) what is truly beneficial and what is not. Our choice to be obedient to God's will for our lives instead of our own plans can clear out all the noise. Then we can clearly hear the promptings of God's Holy Spirit to better pick and choose what to do.

When we choose to trust God at His Word we are able to receive His peace no matter how chaotic the season or circumstance. As that process becomes a regular habit for us, we are more and more able to receive what we need to do each day.

In our super-charged, do-it-all mentality we often forget that there will always be another chore, someone else who needs us, and one more thing to accomplish. We forget that we do not have to be in control of our lives. We forget we do not have to figure everything out. In these times, the idea of letting God have control may be difficult because we are fearful that things will fall apart without us taking care of it. This is faulty thinking because *God is more than capable of taking care of everything* and *He* wants to do it *for* us. Can you imagine, just for a moment, how your life would be different if you daily chose to try and let God direct your life instead of trying to be in charge of all of it?

As I began to try and trust God at His Word, not only did my thinking change but my attitude about my life changed as well. As I went about my day there wasn't this burden of having to get "it" all done and my attitude began to shift from one of rushed impatience to relaxed tolerance. The *circumstances* of my life hadn't changed one bit. I still had crazy kids, struggling finances, and an overwhelming laundry pile. What did change was how I thought about all of it. Slowly, my mental state began to be transformed from one characterized by fear and worry about not being good enough, to one characterized by a complete (although imperfect) trust in the plan of God, regardless of how overwhelming my life became that day.

> "Can you imagine, just for a moment, how your life would be different if you daily chose to try and let God direct your life instead of trying to be in charge of all of it?"

Making time for something new isn't easy to do. Harder still is developing a trust in someone else to be in control. I want you to know this type of change comes from within and works its way out one imperfect choice at a time. I am still experiencing new levels of understanding of what it means to believe God and trust in His promises. What I can tell you is that when I realized I *wanted* God to be in control, that I *wanted* to let Jesus lead me, that I *wanted* to follow where the Holy Spirit guided me, choosing to follow became easier. I still try to plan everything out sometimes, and I still catch myself trying to add in more than I should to my days, but now I recognize sooner when I am doing that and make different choices.

When life gets a bit crazy (and it does) Psalm 46:10, *"Be still and know that I am God,"* often pops into my head and I stop and look to see what, if anything can be eliminated. Then I pray throughout my day... a lot. I am also more willing to slow down when the pace slows down, recognizing that the slow times in life are there for a reason, and I try to take advantage of the rest those seasons offer.

The act of cultivating peace is a lifelong process filled with messy imperfection. Every day I am given the opportunity, however, to learn to trust that God will use all the mistakes I make along the way for my good. (Romans 8:28) There are three things though that I believe are the basic building blocks to this process.

The most important thing we can do to develop our trust in God is to meet with Him EVERY day. Prayer, reflection upon God's word, and waiting upon His direction are essential to cultivating peace. This is what I call "quiet time" and it is unique to each one of us; no two quiet times will, or even should look the same. It doesn't have to be the same time every day, or even the same way. It may sometimes be a quick desperate plea for help and other times may be an extended time of reflection and worship. You may use a Bible or a daily devotional book, write in a journal, listen to podcasts and other digital media, listen to Christian music, or make time to experience nature. The thing to remember is that there is no "right" way to have a quiet time. There will always be reasons *not* to have a quiet time: we are too tired, someone needs us, and there are chores to do. I get that. Allowing God to lead so that we receive His peace means we need to ask Him where we are going. If we don't take the time to find out, we risk continuing to be influenced by the chaos instead of receiving His peace in the midst of it.

> "We all have the same 24 hours every day. What we do with it makes all the difference."

The second thing we need to do is take a good hard look at our current schedules. If your first reaction to having a daily quiet time was "Where will I have the time for that?" you may be in need of a "schedule makeover." If having time in your schedule to regularly do something to help you relax and rejuvenate looks impossible for you, then something definitely needs to change. We all have the same 24 hours every day. What we do with it makes all the difference. When we stop relying on our own understanding and ask God for His, He *will* show us what to do each day in every season. The hard part is actually obeying what He tells us to do. The good news is that we do not have to figure out what to do differently. That's what God wants to do *for* us; He's just waiting for a willing heart to ask Him "How?"

The third thing we need to do is get our priorities in order. *"For where your treasure is, there your heart will be also."* (Matthew 6:21) What do you treasure most? That's where you will spend most of your time. For me, it was in making sure I never let anyone else down; I treasured being needed and so I spent my time making sure I took care of everyone but myself. The result was a stolen life. That's not what God has in mind for you or me. He has a focus for our lives: building relationships. It's in those relationships that God weaves his grace in us and through us so that His love can conquer the obstacles we face. While we all have different relationships in our lives, and they each cycle through different seasons of need, the act of cultivating peace within them builds upon one another in a specific way:

- Develop a relationship with God through salvation in Jesus Christ. (Chapter 1)

- Ask God to reveal to us the truth of who we are and His plans for our life. (Chapters 2 & 4)

- Invite God to nourish and refill us. (Chapter 3)

- Cultivate lasting connections within our marriage relationship and spend time with our husbands. (Chapter 5)

- Teach our children the ways of God and thus develop their character. (Chapter 6)

- Take care to make our homes a safe, peace-filled place. (Chapter 7)

- Use our God-given influence at work (and elsewhere) to honor Him. (Chapter 8)

It all starts with God. He won't let you neglect what's really important. When our lives do not include having a daily quiet time in which we seek to be nourished and led, the effects of the chaos in our lives can begin to overwhelm us. Asking

God to show us how to make changes to our daily schedules in order to get a regular quiet time is essential. Making sure we get our own self-nourishment and refreshment can be a big task, but *"if God is for us, who can be against us?"* (Romans 8:31b) I tell you, our God IS for us in this!

One of the biggest obstacles to making a change is having a place to start. So, in an effort to help you get going, I have gathered together a few activities for your consideration:

1. **Prayer, prayer, prayer!!** Ask for help, clarification, rest…whatever you need most.

2. **Listen for the promptings of the Holy Spirit, and do your best to not ignore them.** Learning to let God lead involves the risk of giving up control. Try it and see how God honors your obedience.

3. **Memorize and meditate on God's Word, one piece of scripture at a time.** A good one to start with is "Be still and know I am God." (Psalm 46:10 NIV, The NASB translates "Be still" as "Cease striving") Try focusing on one word at a time.

4. **Take a break.** Breathe. Shut down for five minutes. Take a quick walk around the office.

5. **Schedule some personal time for yourself.**

6. **Create something.**

7. **Do something nice for someone else.**

8. **Read a great book.**

9. **Have a Girl's Night.**

10. **Join a women's small group or invite other women to join you.**

11. **Spend time in nature.**

No matter what your quiet time looks like, remember its purpose is to nourish you with God's grace, mercy and love, and to strengthen you to face whatever chaos is in your life with a complete trust in God's plans over your own.

Let's pray

Father God, thank You for inviting us into a relationship with You. Please guide us in learning to let You lead us through our days. Teach us how to allow You to nourish us to face the challenges in each day instead of relying upon our own strength. When we find ourselves directed by chaos instead of Your peace, may Your grace cover us and may Your love guide us safely back to where your peace directs. In Jesus' name, Amen.

Be still, and know that I am God

Be **still**, and know that I am God

Be still, **and** know that I am God

Be still, and **know** that I am God

Be still, and know **that** I am God

Be still, and know that **I** am God

Be still, and know that I **am** God

Be still, and know that I am **God**

Psalm 46:10 NIV

Chapter Four
Ripping Out the Weeds

"For though we live in the world, we do not
wage war as the world does. The weapons
we fight with are not the weapons of the world.
On the contrary, they have divine power to
demolish strongholds. We demolish arguments
and every pretension that sets itself up against
the knowledge of God, and we take captive
every thought to make it obedient to Christ."

2 Corinthians 10:3-5 NIV

Four

One morning I sought prayer at our church during one of our weekly Bible studies. Lately, I had been extremely emotional, crying at almost everything which was very unlike my normally controlled self. Truth be told, I always made sure I had it all together. There was no way I would ever give anyone a chance to doubt me, my abilities, or my commitment in any way. To do so would have meant I was a failure, therefore, unlovable because I was imperfect. As I sat there in the presence of women who were praying on my behalf, I was reminded, one after another, of painful instances in my life. The time when my father's comments about my lack of exercise and eating behaviors had made me feel fat, ugly, and unworthy of his love.

Next came a memory of a time when my friend's success at being asked to the prom, while I was forced to ask a boy myself, had made me feel even more unlovable. Then came the time when I had fought with my boyfriend because I wanted more emotional connection from him and he said he wasn't willing to give it to me, again reinforcing the belief that I was unworthy of love from anyone.

However, after each scene played out I heard the words, *"But I loved you."* I knew for sure it was Jesus, but I wondered to Him how I could be loved by Him when it was clear no one else had really loved me. In awe, I watched as each scenario replayed itself through the eyes of Jesus. Through His compassionate, grace-filled eyes my father's comments translated into a deep love for my health and well-being, and I watched as He demolished a chain that had been holding me down to the lie that I was fat. My lack of popularity with boys in high school through the eyes of Jesus translated into protection against heavy social pressures to conform in physical ways that I hadn't been ready to face, and I watched as He destroyed yet another chain that had been holding me down to the lie that I wasn't pretty. My boyfriend's emotional detachment translated into loneliness and a longing for connection which drew me closer to Him and I watched, overcome, as Jesus obliterated a massive chain that had kept me tied to the lie that I wasn't enough, which had kept me from feeling the truth of the everlasting love He had always had for me. Through the eyes of Jesus, I was loved, I was cherished, I was adored. *I became His beloved.* As those images became clearer, as those truths replaced my faulty facts, my perceptions of who I was drastically altered. Who I once had been became undone.

> "...let God transform you into a new person by
> changing the way you think."
> (Romans 12:2b NLT)

What I experienced that morning was an unraveling of a cluster of lies that had held my heart captive. These lies, like so many weeds in a garden, had moved in and taken over. I had lived for years believing the central lie that I was unlovable because my experience had reinforced the lie that I wasn't acceptable the way I was. Additionally, that lie had sprouted others: I was unlovable because I was fat. I was unlovable because I wasn't pretty enough. I was unlovable because I just wasn't good enough.

These lies, what I refer to as "weeds" in our lives, are false thoughts that become beliefs about ourselves the enemy uses to pull us away from God's grace into shame, guilt, fear, envy, self-loathing and other destructive behaviors. No one is exempt from the weeds. They are planted by the chief enemy himself and their sole purpose is to steal God's life-giving Truth in order to take over our garden. Any little thought, any small comment has the potential to get twisted and turned and become a source of so many other lies. We process between 12,000 and 70,000 thoughts *every single day*.[21] 80% of all our thoughts are negative and 98% of all our thoughts are things we have thought before. That's a lot of potential for lies to take root and grow! Think about it. How easy is it to remember that one negative incident in your past? What about that critical comment or that name calling incident? I'll bet you can remember more of those than the positive times, right?

What happens after we take in those negative incidents, comments, and name-callings as truth? They affect our beliefs about ourselves, infecting our ability to see ourselves different-ly. The more we believe a lie, the bigger it's influence on our

> "We process between 12,000 and 70,000 thoughts every single day. 80% of all our thoughts are negative and 98% of all our thoughts are things we have thought before."

lives. Every time a negative thought comes into our heads *and we choose to believe it*, a new belief is born that begins to direct our choices and actions. Because I believed I was fat, for example, I forced myself to strive and fit into an unrealistic ideal of what I thought a "good body" was supposed to look like so I could be lovable. Because I believed I wasn't pretty enough to be asked out by boys, I began to behave in ways that I thought would make me more attractive to them in order to earn their love. Because I believed my need for a deeper emotional connection made me too "needy" I began to hide away the parts of myself that I thought were flawed in order to fit into someone else's ability to love.

> *"Watch your thoughts, for they will become actions. Watch your actions, for they'll become... habits. Watch your habits for they will forge your character. Watch your character, for it will make your destiny."* [22]

One of the biggest ways the lies in our lives are able to spread and infect other areas of our lives is through guilt. *Guilt* is an awareness of having done something wrong, accompanied by feelings of shame and regret that drive us to either hide or fix. When we try to live with guilt we live a limited life. We can become listless and aloof, withdrawing in order to remove any opportunity to "hurt" anyone or mess anything else up, or drained, because we believe we need to make up for the damage we believe we caused. I lived for years under the influence of guilt, for example, because I believed it was *who I was* that made me incapable of being loved. The result was a determination to strive harder to earn others' love. When we live with guilt everything feels as if it's our fault and our responsibility alone to "make right."

Conviction, however, is an awareness of having done something wrong accompanied by the feeling of hope because of God's grace, and a sense of peace because He is stepping in to take over, so that we no longer have to fix or hide away from whatever we thought was our *fault*. Conviction removes the full weight of responsibility off of us and frees us, through God's grace, to receive healing, mercy, and love. While those women prayed over me, the Holy Spirit convicted me that how I had been seeing the events in my past wasn't the truth, and restored my hope in who I was by revealing God's truth to me, lavishing me with His grace.

Trying to live in God's peace while lies control our thoughts, beliefs, and actions is like trying to plant a beautiful garden without first clearing out the land on which we want to plant. I wanted a relationship with Jesus. I wanted to accept God's truth about who I was to Him, and to believe His Word as truth in my life, but the weeds choked out all of that. I wasn't feeling any peace, not because Jesus wasn't close to me, but because the lies in my head were acting as a barrier, a stronghold if you will, against being able to receive His presence. It wasn't until I invited Jesus to show me His truth, and *chose to stop believing everything I thought*, that I began to be freed from those lies. As I did I began to taste

"What lies have you been living with? Where are you living with the belief that you aren't enough: aren't smart enough, pretty enough, thin enough, perfect enough?"

89

the true peace Jesus had waiting for me all along.

Weeds are difficult to recognize and dig out because they come quietly into our gardens, often from simple little comments repeated in different ways over the course of years. Others come crashing into our gardens, often screamed at us, blatantly exposing our insecurities and fears. All lies have the same effect, though. They make us want to hide our "imperfect" selves away behind a mask of whatever we use to cover our wounds, building up strongholds of self-protection. What lies have you been living with? Where are you living with the belief that you aren't enough: aren't smart *enough*, pretty *enough*, thin *enough*, perfect *enough*?

Eleanor Roosevelt has been quoted as saying: "No one can make you feel inferior without your consent."[23] Also true is that no one can make you feel unloved, fat, ugly, overworked, or any anything else without your consent. We allow the weeds, no matter how they got there, to flourish in our lives when we choose to believe any voice that tells us we aren't worthy enough *just as we are* to be cherished, valued, or accepted, or any voice that make us feel ashamed, guilty, or condemned.

"The thief comes to steal and kill and destroy..." (John 10:10a NLT) Yes, he does.

Let me tell you something, though. The truth is that you don't have to believe any of those negative thoughts fueled by guilt, shame, and condemnation any longer. You can choose to stop believing everything you think.

First, we can ask God to help us *recognize* that we are living with lies. We can invite Him into the areas of our lives that are filled with pain, shame, guilt, and frustration. Areas where we believe we are failures and areas where the pain is too deep to even admit to another person. These are the places where the lies take root and every relationship we are in can be affected by them, especially the relationships we have with God and ourselves.

"Looking at those areas of hurt, pain, shame, or guilt through God's eyes gives us the opportunity to recognize the lies and receive healing."

When we invite God into those places and He reveals to us the lies we have been living with as a result of those times, we are able to get to the heart of where the lies took root and are able to more effectively allow Him to clean them out. Think of it like this. When you go out to clear the weeds in your garden, if you don't grab the whole thing--roots and all--it usually comes back, right? Well, the lies in our hearts act the same way. When we allow God to take us to the root cause of the lie, we can more fully understand not only how it got there, but also see the truth of the situation surrounding its placement. Looking at those areas of hurt, pain, shame, or guilt through God's eyes gives us the opportunity to recognize the lies and receive healing.

Second, *replacing* those lies with the truth of God's Word is what establishes our freedom from them. *"Every part of Scripture is God-breathed and useful one way or another— showing us truth, exposing our rebellion, correcting our mistakes, training us to live God's way. Through the Word, we are put together and shaped up for the tasks God has for us."* (2 Timothy 3:16-17 the VOICE) When we not only recognize a lie but replace it with a *belief in the truth of God's word* over the lie, we are freed, one negative thought at a time, from the lies we are living with. Learning to trust God at His word is like covering our gardens with weed block after we have cleared out the weeds so that they cannot come back: it creates a barrier that further protects us so that we more consistently live *"the rich and satisfying life"* Jesus came to give us. (John 10:10b NLT)

Third, as we more readily invite God to help us recognize those lies, and make the choice to replace them by believing God's truth instead of the lie, we engage with God in resisting their presence in our lives. Ephesians 6:16 tells us that our enemy will hurl flaming arrows at us.[24] This is his main job and he never ceases from it. Our faith in God's Word, however, activates our protection and we are given the ability to see the lies for what they are before they can take root in our belief system, therefore *resisting* them not in our own strength, but in His. Just as we might go out and spray weed-b-gone on a regular basis so that the weeds cannot take over the plants of our gardens, learning to recognize the lies we are living with gives us the ability to spot them and replace them with the Truth as many times as we need to. This process gains more power the more we use it. As we learn to recognize the lies in our lives, and learn how to trust God's word instead, more and more lies come to the surface to be ripped out and replaced with the Truth. As we engage with God in this process we are, by the very act of ripping out the weeds, resisting new ones from coming in.

There are many, many lies that I have uncovered in my own life. Some were easy to spot and remove, but many more were deeply rooted in the woman I had grown to be. Removing them has proven to be challenging. At first I didn't see the lies, though. I just told myself that I wasn't good enough and strove to work harder at doing things "right enough" to be loved and accepted. Sometimes I would decide that things in my life weren't going smoothly because of someone else's behavior as well, blaming others' lack of commitment, dedication, or willingness to do things right.

As a result, I lived suspended between constant fear and instant anger. My behavior was erratic, alternating between reaching out for love and acceptance, and shoving away those around me in disappointment. I was living the tumultuous experience of trying to live a peaceful life overrun with weeds. I constantly yelled, slammed doors, and muttered utterances under my breath. I dreamed-up fights I could win in my head, complained constantly, argued about everything, and manipulated those around me all in an effort to maintain control. The little glimpses of peace I might have been able to receive in building a relationship with Jesus and asking God to nourish me with His "super soil" were soon overshadowed by the coping behaviors I used in my daily life. I was living a life of turmoil, controlled by the chief thief himself, instead of the full life that Jesus came to give.

When I first began to follow God's plan for my life I didn't want to believe I had been living with lies. I just wanted things to get better. But, as I spent time in prayer and in the Word, I felt the Holy Spirit remind me over and over that my reactions and behaviors were not the ones God wanted me to have. I couldn't shake those behaviors on my own. No matter how hard *I* tried to change I was completely inconsistent. However, *when I stopped trying to fix myself* and asked God to step in and help me understand why I couldn't change, I came to understand that until the weeds were removed, until the lies were examined and replaced with God's truth, the relationships in my life, especially my relationships with Jesus, myself, my husband, and my kids would continue to be infected. I wanted to have beautiful, healthy relationships in all areas of my life. So, I chose to invite God in to dig out each lie one by one.

Inviting God to help us recognize, replace, and resist the lies in our lives is a process we can actively engage in. Yes, *His* power is what frees us, but our willing participation in that process is a necessary component. Our key scripture for this chapter uses the verb "take" in its present tense form. We are to work *with* God to *"take captive"* the thoughts in our heads and *"make them obedient to Christ."* How do we do this? How do we invite God in to guide us and participate with Him?

Take a look at Ephesians 6:10-18 (NLT):

*"Be strong in the Lord and in his mighty power. Put on all of God's armor so that you will be able to stand firm against all strategies of the devil. For we are not fighting against flesh-and-blood enemies, but against evil rulers and authorities of the unseen world, against mighty powers in this dark world, and against evil spirits in the heavenly places. Therefore, **put on every piece of God's armor so you will be able to resist the enemy in the time of evil**. Then after the battle you will still be standing firm. Stand your ground, putting on the belt of truth and the body armor of God's righteousness. For shoes, put on the peace that comes from the Good News so that you will be fully prepared. In addition to all of these, hold up the shield of faith to stop the fiery arrows of the devil. Put on salvation as your helmet, and take*

the sword of the Spirit, which is the word of God."

There are two major truths in these verses that I want to focus on.

First, God has made available to us both offensive and defensive weapons to use in our battle against the weeds:

Defensive Weapons:

The Belt of Truth (verse 14): Our defense against the enemy's accusations that we aren't good enough, strong enough, worthy enough, or *(your struggle here)* enough. The Truth of God's Word functions as a filter to help us recognize what is true and what is a lie. If it doesn't match God's Word, it's a lie.[25]

The Breastplate of Righteousness (verse 14): Our protection against the accusations the enemy tries to hurl at our hearts. When we accepted the free gift of salvation in Jesus Christ, we were made righteous in God's eyes. We ARE enough.[26]

The Shoes of Peace (verse 15): Our defense against retreating and hiding away from facing the challenges in our lives. These shoes remind us of the Good News that we have all we need in Jesus. This opens the door of our fear-filled hearts to be flooded with peace so that we remain rooted on our new foundation.[27]

The Shield of Faith (verse 16): Our defense against things like doubt, guilt, hopelessness, and despair. These feelings are the tools the enemy uses to keep us from growing. When we choose to believe the promises of God, we hold our shields high and prevent Satan's arrows (verse 16) from penetrating our hearts.[28]

The Helmet of Salvation (verse 17): Our defense against getting confused or listening to illogical thinking which tells us that our salvation is not enough to clean us of all our sins--past, present, and future.[29]

Offensive Weapon:

The Sword of the Spirit (verse 17): This one is my personal favorite because it is the very weapon Jesus uses when He is tempted by the devil's false thinking in the desert (Luke 4:1-13 NIV), and what He will use to defeat Satan once and for all when He returns (Revelation 19:11-21 NIV). This sword is also known as the "rhema" or spoken word of God. When we recite Scripture aloud, like a sword it cuts through the enemy's attempts to lie to us.[30]

Second, choosing to put on our armor is what protects us. Take a look at verses 11 and 13: *"Put on all of God's armor so that you will be able to stand firm against all strategies of the devil. ... Therefore, put on every piece of God's armor so you will be able to resist the enemy in the time of evil. Then after the battle you will still be standing firm."* We are to **put our armor on** and receive the strength to stand against the lies of the enemy. God will do the rest.

When I first read these verses I imagined myself fitted with a warrior's armor (dented in places from attacks no doubt), standing with my shield on my right arm, and my sword raised high in my left hand. My feet were firmly planted on the ground, legs crouching against the attack. I used to believe I was engaging in battle alone, digging out the lies, defending against new ones. I felt hopelessly engaged in a never-ending battle for God's truth to reign in my life. Every day was a battle in which I would continue to search for just the right thing to say and do. Peace was something to be sought out, manipulated into being, planned for, and I was going to make sure I had it. Do you know what happened? I grew weary over and over and over again.

When I recognized the truth that all I needed to do was stand (verses 11 and 13) and Jesus Christ Himself would step in and battle *for* me, I more fully understood the power in the Armor of God. Look again at each of our weapons. None of them require us to do more than allow God to put them on us and hold to our resolve to trust God at His Word. We are to trust, have faith, and stand, firmly holding to our beliefs when the attacks come.

This is more than just thinking differently. This involves planting ourselves firmly on the Rock of our salvation and choosing to believe essential truths about ourselves. Truths such as **we are daughters of The King:** *"But for all who did receive and trust in Him, He gave them the right to be reborn as children of God."* (John 1: 12 the VOICE) That **we have been forgiven:** *"Then Jesus said to her, "Your sins are forgiven."* (Luke 7:48 NIV) **redeemed and restored to a right relationship with God:** *"Christ redeemed us from the curse of the law by becoming a curse for us..."* (Galatians 3:13a NIV) and **nothing can ever separate us from the love of Christ:** *"For I am convinced that neither death nor life, neither angels nor demons, neither the present nor the future, nor any powers, neither height nor depth, nor anything else in all creation, will be able to separate us from the love of God that is in Christ Jesus our Lord.* (Romans 8:38-39 NIV). When those truths become our root-base, we can begin to see everything in our lives differently. We see that the

> "Will you choose to put your armor on? Will you choose to invite God into every part of your heart in order to uncover the lies you have been living with?"

thoughts that bombard us, from the messages in the world to the messages from those we know, don't match what we know to be true and we begin to take captive every thought and make it obedient to what Jesus says instead of just taking it at face value.

This process is not a "once and we're done" activity. Some lies will come out easily and never return, but some, usually those that are rooted deep among several areas of our life, are the hardest to both fully identify and to dig out. Sometimes when we have identified and dug out a root, it will try to come back again and again. But, we don't battle in our own strength and this power doesn't come from something we create on our own; it comes directly from God himself so that we are free to simply experience it and the freedom it creates for us. (Remember the first part of this chapter where Jesus destroyed the chains that had held me down?)

Then when we miss a thought or get caught up in arguments in our heads again (and we will) it isn't something we need to beat ourselves up for. Instead, it becomes a reason to draw closer to God and receive His restoration, a reason to praise Him for His grace in our lives.

Will you choose to put your armor on? Will you choose to invite God into every part of your heart in order to uncover the lies you have been living with?

• • •

On my quest to understand how to break free from the lies I was living with I read a book called <u>Lies Women Believe, and the Truth That Sets Them Free</u>.[31] It was the first time I had ever heard of the concept of using God's Word to replace the lies I'd been living with in order to be freed from them. Each weed I have listed below is a lie I myself have struggled with along with the truth that has helped me. I share them with you in hopes that they might serve as a starting place from which you might allow Jesus to begin His weed-removal process in your life.

Lie #1
God is not really enough?[32]

(I have to do it all or it won't get done.) Psalm 23:1 tells us that God will make sure we are taken care of: *"The Lord is my shepherd; I shall not be in want."* When I look at my life through the words of this verse I recognize that my struggle to "do it all" precluded God from helping me. Because I didn't trust that anyone would be there to help I denied the fact that God says I will not be in want...for help, or support, or anything. Once I began to look at each "do it all" situation as an opportunity for God to show me His way, I began to trust Him and quit trying to control it all. That is when I received His peace that things would work out *without my having to figure out how.*

Lie #2
Submission will lead to misery.

(If I submit, I will lose my identity.) Proverbs 21:1 (The Message) states that submission places us under God-ordained authority, accepting that He is bigger and more knowledgeable than us: *"Good leadership is a channel of water controlled by God; he directs it to whatever ends he chooses."* I initially didn't believe this truth. For some reason, I loved being in control. Maybe it was because I needed to have importance in my life. Maybe it was to hide my insecurities. It may even have been to say I was doing everything in a martyr sort of way. Either way the word "submission" left a nasty taste in my mouth because of my need to be in control. Once I chose to follow Jesus though, I realized how weary trying to be in control had made me. It was one of my chief peace-stealers. When I accepted that God was bigger than I, that He knew more about my life than I did, I had peace about submitting to His plan for my life.

Lie #3
I am not fully responsible for my actions and reactions.

(I expect those around me to make me happy.) Philippians 4:8-9 reminds us, *"Finally brothers, whatever is true, whatever is noble, whatever is right, whatever is pure, whatever is lovely, whatever is admirable—if anything is excellent or praiseworthy—think about such things. Whatever you have learned or received or heard from me, or seen in me— put it into practice. And the God of peace will be with you."* However, because of this weed of expectation, I looked to other people and things to make me happy. I was often surrounded, however, by people who were in needy places. Thus, I worked to make sure they were happy so that I could be happy. It sounds so messed up, I know, but that is what living with weeds does to us—it clouds our thinking. Once I recognized this weed I began asking God to help me focus on my own life and making the changes I needed to make. This also meant I had to let go of being responsible for making those around me happy too, which was hard at first.[33] The more I stuck with this verse, the more peace I had.

Lie #4
I shouldn't have to suffer.

(I deserve to be happy.) Hebrews 2:18 reminds us of Jesus' suffering and how He will help us through our trials. *"Because he himself suffered when he was tempted, he is able to help those who are being tempted."* It was hard at first to recognize this attitude as a weed. Many of the mature Christians I observed never seemed to be stressed out, worried, or chaotic like I was. I thought they were free from trouble because they were saved and therefore protected from tragedy. I wondered what was wrong with me. As I grew in my knowledge of God and His Word, however, I came to realize that as Christ-followers we are no more exempt from suffering than anyone else.

But there is a difference for us. We have a choice in how to handle the suffering that comes our way. We can trust in ourselves and our own plan or turn to God for help. Those mature Christians had developed the habit of turning to God through experiencing many, many trials. They followed Him through the situation, rather than following their own plan around it. When I sought to do the same I found peace in suffering. It wasn't that the suffering went away or lessened, I simply had peace in it from believing that God would walk me through it and bring me safely to the other side.

Lie #5
I have my rights.

(I determine how to spend my time.) Claiming my own individual rights set me up in opposition to Psalm 37:11: *"The meek will inherit the land and enjoy great peace."* As a recovering control-freak, this weed was a tough one to let go. When I remained in control I knew what was going to happen every minute (or at least I told myself that). Yet, I was stressed-out all the time. My response was to try and control everything *better*, but that never worked for long. When I decided to "give-in" (that's how I saw it at first) and let God be in control instead, I ended up not only having less stress but more time to do what needed to be done. When I listened to His voice telling me to relax, for example, He has given me enough time to get my household chores done. When I obeyed His plans to be with my kids, there was always enough time to do the errands I had planned. In short, when I lived the priorities He had for my life, I had peace.

Lie #6
I don't have the time to do everything I am supposed to do.

(Expecting my family or others to help me achieve all I want to do.) Ephesians 2:10 reminds us that there is plenty of time to do what God intends for us to do: *"For we are God's workmanship, created in Christ Jesus to do good works, which God prepared in advance for us to do."* When my life was at its busiest points my anger always flared at my husband when he just chilled out and relaxed. (Especially during football season!) I wondered, *"How could he sit there and relax when I had so much to do. Didn't he care about me? Didn't he want to help?"* You bet we had many, many fights over that one point. During one such time of intense fellowship my husband uttered, "You can relax too, you know! You don't have to always do everything. You wouldn't have to if you said 'no' once in a while."

I think it's so funny sometimes who God speaks through, don't you? That afternoon as I licked my proverbial wounds, I realized that my husband was right. I had been saying yes to too many things and expecting him to help me pick up the slack. That's the problem with trying to live life according to the world rather than according to God's plan for us. I began to recognize that most of my "yes's" to others' requests for my time and energy had been to please them without considering what God wanted from me first. When I checked in with God before answering, the result was peace in each decision I made and the ability to keep up with the pace.

Lie #7

If my circumstances were different I would be different.

(Expecting everyone to do things my way.) Luke 6:45 reminds us that we are not made by our circumstances but revealed through them, *"The good man brings good things out of the good stored up in his heart, and the evil man brings out the evil stored up in his heart. For out of the overflow of his heart his mouth speaks."* My circumstances were revealing that I was a self-centered, scared, over-scheduled mess! It was not a pretty picture. As much as I tried to change things in order to feel more peace (or at least less stress), I still found myself reverting to anger, yelling, and slamming doors. My heart was not stocked with good things because of the weeds.

Once I allowed God to examine my heart and saw how much fear covered all my decisions and reactions, I realized I couldn't change until I dealt with that fear. Like the weed of control, I soon realized that the weed of fear was attached to many other weeds in my life. (Truth be told, I am still digging up pieces of this weed.) Peace comes when I face what I am afraid of (remember we are to stand firm once we put our armor on) and trust God to take care of things. Because I have the assurance that God will be there, my heart is now stocked with good things like trust, perseverance, and hope. In addition, my angry outbursts resulting from fear are occurring less and less.

• • •

Realizing that we have been living under the control of lies can be overwhelming, but the good news is that we are not alone in getting caught up in a lie. The Bible tells us of several women, like Eve and Abraham's Sarah, who believed lies and took matters into their own hands, thus causing difficulty in their lives as a result. It also tells of men like David who did the same thing. These Biblical figures suffered greatly for their decisions to live their lives on their own terms. Eve is credited with the fall of all mankind. (Genesis 3) Sarah encouraged her husband to commit adultery and then forced him to exile the son of that union. (Genesis 15-16) David caused Bathsheba to commit adultery and then arranged to murder her husband to cover his sin. (2 Samuel 11) There were some huge weeds growing in their gardens!

Restoration, however, came to each of them, and it can come to us too. Eve's choice is used as a guidepost for us today, saving millions of women like us from following Satan's lies for too long. God's promise to Sarah was fulfilled with the birth of her son Isaac. David turned to the Lord in repentance and is still recognized as one of the most faith-filled men of all time.

God showed each of these historical figures how to clear out the weeds in their lives and start over on the design He had planned from the start. He wants to do the same thing for us! In gardening, when a large weed is removed there is a hole left where its roots once were. It's the same in our hearts: when we remove the lies that have strangled us, the hole that's left needs to be filled. That's where the truth comes in. There is a garden waiting for you underneath all the weeds, but it cannot be cultivated without first removing what overran it in the first place. Take some time to search the Bible for your truths. If you are unsure where to start, check out available resources at your local Christian bookstore or look for specific words in the concordance found at the back of your Bible.

Fortunately, we do not have to rely on *"our own understanding"* (Proverbs 3:6) to remove the weeds. We have Holy Help. The Bible states in John 14:26, *"But the Counselor, the Holy Spirit whom the Father will send in my name will teach you all things and will remind you of everything I have said to you."* How do we know when we are hearing from the Counselor himself? Remember our definitions of "guilt" and "conviction?" The Holy Spirit grants us **conviction** -- a hope that things can change not condemnation when we have followed a lie. He also grants us gifts as we learn to live with Truth instead of lies. Galatians 5:19-22 reminds us that *"...the fruit of the Spirit is love, joy, peace, patience, kindness, goodness, faithfulness, gentleness, and self-control..."* The Holy Spirit comes to help us navigate our days on purpose for God, not ourselves. When we are living by the direction of the Holy Spirit, our emotional state will reflect it.

The amazing thing is that even if we are experiencing the effects of a life filled with weeds we can claim the fruits of the Spirit right now. We can leave behind all the anger, frustration, envy, and pain, and have them replaced by peace and joy. When we choose to be mindful of God's presence throughout our day, *to daily ask Him what he wants us to do, how to do it, and wait for His answer,* we can be rewarded with an overwhelming, powerful, and beautiful sense of peace no matter how deep the roots of our weeds go. The only requirement is that we continue to choose to let go of the control of our lives and trust that God's way is better. He can *"do immeasurably more than all we ask or imagine according to his power that is at work within us."* (Ephesians 3:20)

Satan has been a deceiver and a liar from the moment he fell from grace. He will always seek to make you feel unworthy, but he can NEVER win! All he can do is try to make us feel something and act on those feelings until the day he is destroyed. Jesus came so we could have life and have it to the full. He has already won and so have all who claim Him as their Savior. Amen!

Let's Pray:

Father God, thank You for Your armor to help us stand firmly in faith against the lies of the enemy. Thank You for Your Word which reminds us of the truth. Thank You for the Holy Spirit who guides us each day along the path You have marked out for us. Please help us to trust You more today than we did yesterday. Please help us to recognize the lies we are living with that keep us from living the joyously abundant life Your Son Jesus came to give us. Amen

The thief comes only to steal, kill, and destroy;
I have come that they may have life, and have it to the full."
John 10:10 NIV

Part Two

Cultivating Peace in Relationships

"In your relationships with one another,
have the same mindset as Christ Jesus:
Who, being in very nature God, did not
consider equality with God something to be
used to his own advantage; rather, he made
himself nothing by taking the very nature of
a servant, being made in human likeness.
And being found in appearance as a man,
he humbled himself by becoming obedient
to death—even death on a cross! Therefore
God exalted him to the highest place and gave
him the name that is above every name,
that at the name of Jesus every knee should
bow, in heaven and on earth and under the
earth, and every tongue acknowledge that
Jesus Christ is Lord, to the glory
of God the Father."

Philippians 2:5-11 NIV

Chapter Five

Cultivating Peace in Marriage

"Haven't you read that in the beginning
God created humanity male and female?
Don't you remember what the story of
our creation tells us about marriage?
'For this reason, a man will leave his
mother and father and cleave to his wife,
and the two shall become one flesh.'"

Matthew 19:4-5 the VOICE

Five

Marriage. This one word is loaded with so much expectation, isn't it?

My husband and I dated for eight years before finally getting married. We met when we were 18 and freshmen in college, and continued dating until we were both established in our careers and our college debt was paid off. During those eight years I dreamed a lot about our wedding day. I bought wedding magazines to determine the style of wedding dress I would wear and flowers I would have. I bought a book on wedding venues in the Bay Area to choose where we would get married. I even bought a guide on how to plan a perfect wedding. I spent weeks choosing appropriate wedding registry items. I spent months planning out the food and seating arrangements and honeymoon. Not once, however, did I think about the days after our wedding day.

I remember the evening my husband and I met with the pastor we had hired to perform our ceremony (he came recommended from a friend since neither of us attended church or even knew a pastor). I distinctly remember telling him I did not want him to mention God at all during our ceremony and that the part in the vows about "love, honor, and obey" was not going to be a part of our ceremony; I wasn't going to obey anyone. I am not sure what he thought about us, but on the day of our wedding, true to his higher commitment, he did ask God to bless our marriage. I am not sure we would have survived if he hadn't called on God to watch over us *for* us.

Since our wedding day we have had many, many fights. While we had dated for eight years, we hadn't taken time to really get to know each other from the standpoint of our values and beliefs about marriage. We each brought hurts, hang-ups and imperfections to our relationship, but since neither one of us had ever dealt with any of them, we had no idea how to help each other. In our own ways we each expected the other to complete us. What that created was a state of marital conflict, not wedded bliss. In the years that followed, there would be more chaos than peace, no matter how hard we worked.

I have come to realize that I entered into my marriage with all kinds of expectations and ideas about how a good one should look. Unfortunately, those beliefs were based mostly on my own understanding of marriage formed by watching both broken marriages and false marriages portrayed in books and on television. This created an unreal ideal that I strove to make a reality. The majority of the conflict that resulted in our marriage came because each of us had expectations and ideals that were in direct opposition (sometimes) to one another. Neither of us had a way to navigate through those expectations without feeling like somehow one of us was not valued by the other. Years spent trying to live up to our own ideals caused so much hurt in our marriage, from both of us. I manipulated. My husband shut down. We both sought out unhealthy ways to deal with what we believed were the failures we were to each other.

Marriage is hard. Bringing two individuals together to form "one flesh" in peace is nearly impossible in our own strength and I have the battle scars to prove it. I am sure you have some of your own as well. What began as an incredible gift from our Creator was one of the first things tainted by sin. That stain has lingered in all marriages since the Fall.[34]

I feel compelled to stop here and point out something important: if you are in an abusive marriage of any form, put down this book and please consider contacting the National Domestic Abuse Hotline (1-800-799-SAFE (7233) or www.thehotline.org), a Christian counselor, or your pastor for guidance immediately. This situation is dangerous and detrimental to all facets of your well-being. It requires professional help and separation from the abuse. This book in no way is meant to speak to the wounds of such a marriage. While my heart goes out to you, I am in no way qualified to share any instruction on how to cultivate peace in an abusive marriage.

Aside from abuse then, how do we cultivate peace in our marriage? It starts with acknowledging that our marriages are not just a union of two. The act of making a covenant promise in marriage begins with God's promise to *us*.[35] Even if we choose not to acknowledge Him, He is with *us* always. When we get married then, we become one flesh with our husbands, but under the influence of God himself.

Imagine a triangle pointing up:[36]

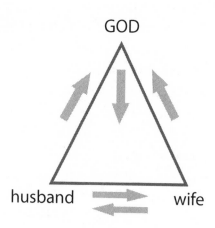

Notice that there are several arrows: up from the husband and wife to God, down from God to us, and across from the husband and wife to the other. The more we turn to God, the more He pours out on us. The more we receive from God, the more we are able to pour out on our spouse. I am a better wife when I seek to honor God *first*. My husband is a better husband when he seeks to honor God first as well. Our marriage is made better the more we each seek to honor God. Because of sin we are not capable of loving each other well without Him. He does not condemn us for not being able to create peace-filled marriages on our own, but He helps us have a marriage beyond anything we could ask for or imagine *when we let Him show us what that looks like instead of trying to create it for ourselves.*

Like our personal lives, our marriage relationship can be overrun with weeds. We each bring faulty thinking, impossible expectations, fears, and worries into every relationship we enter into. Part One of this book was a lesson in how to allow

God to cultivate peace within our own lives, but it also serves as a blueprint for how to allow Him to cultivate peace in each of the relationships in our lives as well. Our transformation from chaos to peace continues with identifying which beliefs in our marriages are weeds and replacing them with God's truth, just as we did in our own personal lives.

While we all may have different weeds in our marriages, there are two unifying truths about this special relationship. The first truth about marriage is that we cannot change our husbands; all we can change is ourselves. Matthew 7:3-5 (The VOICE) states: *"Why is it that you see the dust in your brother's or sister's eye, but you can't see what is in your own eye? Don't ignore the wooden plank in your eye, while you criticize the speck of sawdust in your brother's eyelashes. That type of criticism and judgment is a sham! Remove the plank from your own eye, and then perhaps you will be able to see clearly how to help your brother flush out his sawdust."* Each one of our own sinful ways constitutes a separate "wooden plank." Think of them as the weeds we allowed to grow in our gardens. The outward appearance of these weeds can come in a variety of ways; over-controlling behavior, unrealistic expectations, a lack of respect for our husbands, personal sinfulness (i.e. our own infidelity, addictions, etc.), and exhibiting behaviors of an enabling personality. When we don't deal with our own "planks," and instead nag our husbands to work on theirs, we enter into hypocrisy.

I can hear some of you shouting, "Why do I have to be the one to deal with this? Why can't *he* do something?" I have screamed those same accusatory questions at God hundreds of times. I wish I could tell you He agreed with me and immediately went to work on my husband, but He didn't. I have come

> "I can't change my husband, but I can choose to ask God to heal me of the hurts and help me be the wife He created me to be in our marriage."

to believe that He wants the best marriage possible for the both of us; however, we each have to make our own decision to choose to trust Him with what that looks like. I can't change my husband, but I can choose to ask God to heal me of the hurts and help me be the wife He created me to be in our marriage.

Since you are here, looking for peace within your marriage, He has called you to be the one to make the changes… for now. We can be assured that working on our own planks will result in changes in our marriage, even if our husbands do not make the same decision. God has brought about more changes in my husband as a result of my obedience to Him than I ever could on my own. The toughest step is *to decide to try and follow God's lead* in your marriage and to allow Him to mold you into the wife He created you to be.

The second unifying truth is that all marriages require a love that is beyond our human capabilities. This type of love is known as **Agape** love. Agape love is not like the love we feel in friendship, nor is it physical love. It is the love that is of and from God, perfected in representation through the Trinity. *God* sent His Son in love. The Son, *Jesus*, shows us how to love by both sacrificing Himself for us and by telling us how much God loves us. He sent *The Holy Spirit* to continually remind us of how much we are loved so that we could love one another as we ourselves have been loved. They all operate together in our lives as *One* (the Trinity) to help us receive love. Once we have received that love, our command from God is to love one another, including our husbands. *"Jesus replied, "'You must love the Lord your God with all your heart, all your soul, and all your mind.' This is the first and greatest commandment. A second is equally important: 'Love your neighbor as yourself.'"* (Matthew 22:37-39 NLT)

Our willingness to submit to God comes from an out-flowing of the love we first received from Him in His sacrifice of Jesus Christ *for us.* The first part of this book was designed to help you recognize a need for that love and to hopefully accept the free gift of that love. Our marriages are greatly affected when we choose to receive that love because it gives us the ability to love our spouse with God's mercy and grace.

All of us struggle in marriage at one time or another. We are two distinct individuals with our own strengths and weaknesses, gifts and talents, personality types and love languages. There will be conflict. How we handle those conflicts to a great degree can determine the longevity of our marriages. When bitterness, resentment, and hurt build up it may be that the only thing we can see to do is to end them and walk away. But we do have another choice. We can choose to invite God into our marriages instead and let Him show us what to do.

I have had to make such a choice. I was at my limit and ready to walk away. Years of bitterness and resentment and loneliness all came together and all I could see was that my life would be better if I just left. To this day, I do not know what kept me from calling a lawyer and ending my marriage. Instead, I broke down and offered up a cry for help, a desperate plea to God to make

> "Cultivating peace in marriage is based on making the choice to allow God to transform us from the wife we are today into the wife He created us to be for the marriage we are in."

it work for me. With that act of submission, God began the process of transforming *me* to be the wife He created me to be, which *in part* has led to the restoration of my marriage. I believe He wants to transform you as well, but personal transformation is not a guarantee for a revived marriage. I firmly believe that restoring a marriage takes the willingness of the husband **and** the wife, as well as the presence and power of God. A marriage takes two people and a divorce means that at least one person was not willing to make it work. What happens as a result of your submission to God's will is between you and God and His plans for your life. If it's reconciliation and restoration, with God's help you can learn to trust and love each other again. If it's divorce, with God's help you can receive healing, offer forgiveness, and build a new life with God as your husband until He provides a different plan.

•   •   •

No matter where your marriage lies on the spectrum of personal happiness and fulfillment, we can learn to receive God's peace in the midst of the chaos. Cultivating peace in marriage is based on making the choice to allow God to transform us from the wife we are today into the wife He created us to be for the marriage we are in. Since we are each uniquely created by God, no two of us will live out this role in the same way, and that is as it should be. However, we are ALL called to be our husband's helper. *"The Lord God said, 'it is not good for man to be alone. I will make a helper suitable for him'"* (Genesis 2:18). What can this look like? Martha Peace, in her book <u>The Excellent Wife</u>, describes it like this:

"God's will for every Christian wife is that her most important ministry be to her husband. After a wife's own personal relationship with the Lord Jesus Christ, nothing else should have greater priority. Her husband should be the primary benefactor of his wife's time and energy, not the recipient of what may be left over at the end of the day. Whether her husband is a faithful Christian man, or an unbeliever, God wants every Christian woman to become a godly wife."[37]

If you're anything like me, the preceding quote almost sent you right over the edge. I know when I first read those few sentences I thought about tossing the book out the window and going back to doing things my own way. You may be feeling completely overwhelmed at this point, and I don't blame you one bit. If this is the first time you have ever thought about marriage like this, it can be rather unsettling. When I am feeling overwhelmed, I find it beneficial to break down the expectations into doable steps. In trying to become Godly wives I believe this is especially necessary. That is why we are looking at cultivating peace in marriage through the process of the individualized smaller action steps of submission, respect, forgiveness, and intimacy.

Submission

"*Submit to one another out of reverence for Christ. Wives, submit to your husbands as to the Lord. For the husband is the head of the wife, as Christ is the head of the church, his body, of which he is the Savior. Now as the church submits to Christ, so also wives should submit to their husbands in everything. Husbands, love your wives, just as Christ loved the church and gave himself up for her…This is the profound mystery—but I am talking about Christ and the church. However, each one of you also must love his wife as he loves himself, and the wife must respect her husband.*" (Ephesians 5:21-25, 32-33 NIV)

This passage often creates unrest and resentment in women because it blatantly tells us we are to allow our husbands to be our leader and we are to respect them for it as well. That is often a hard pill to swallow if our husbands do not behave in a manner worthy of respect or if we are filled with bitterness and anger. However, let's look at the passage in more detail.

"If we start with the beginning of the passage, Ephesians 5:21, we see that **all people** are called to submit to one another for the sake of Christ—husbands, wives, children, singles…Christ has paid the ultimate sacrifice to save us, and we love him for it. Therefore, we willingly submit to our brothers and sisters in the Lord out of that **love**. *(This is not a worldly love, but rather Agape love, which I discussed above).* We love and submit because Christ first loved us. In the same way, in the marriage relationship, **the beginning of the equation is not submission, but love**. A husband's loving interaction with his wife will produce a willing submission to him. **A wife's**

loving interaction with her husband will produce tender leadership on his part. Submission does not mean women become wimpy, doormat wives. **Submission requires an inner strength to obey God** and willingly submit to one's husband. It means fulfillment and esteem in the godly role of a wife."[38] (Boldness and italicization are mine.)

We are not learning how to submit for our husband's sakes; we are doing it *for* God. We also are not being asked to do it in our own strength. The power of the Holy Spirit, God's power, is working within us to give us the necessary self-control, physical availability, and/or emotional strength to submit.

Submission to my husband was wholly unnatural to me. Growing up there was no consistent model of male leadership in my life. There were plenty of female dominant models, however, so I never actually believed men were supposed to lead, or at least they couldn't lead as effectively as women. I also didn't feel my husband deserved to be in charge, and my take-control attitude often got in the way. At first my husband was uncomfortable with the idea that I was coming to him to make the decisions for our family. It was difficult to get him to make a decision. Additionally I feared that submitting to him would mean losing my identity and any source of power I might have in our relationship. However, just the opposite became true. The more I asked for his plans and decision in everyday matters, the more he wanted to hear my views. Often, my views became his because there was no nagging or bullying on my part. Other times, he would have a completely different view, but I would do what he asked, trusting God to work everything out, or

"Submission in marriage is about letting go of being in control of how things are to turn out, and instead letting God work them out through our husband's leadership, supported by our knowledge and experience."

to walk with my husband through the consequences.

It's important to note here that the process of learning to allow my husband to lead continues to this day and has been filled with all kinds of messes and additional conflicts. He often chooses to do (or not do) things that I feel should be done. He doesn't make decisions like I do. His personality prefers to "wait and see" while mine prefers to try and keep the worst-case scenario from ever happening. There have been many times when I have had to watch, mouth shut, as the things I knew would happen came to pass because he didn't listen to me. But God. He knows my heart is to follow Him. So, while there have been many times I have argued in my head with Him about why He didn't make my husband listen to me, He has been faithful to work all things for my good, my husband's good, and the good of our marriage. Submission in marriage is about letting go of being in control of how things are to turn out, and instead letting God work them out through our husband's leadership, supported by our knowledge and experience.

I know the idea of submission is not easy to hear. I believe it's because the enemy is trying to hold us down. He has taken the hurts we have felt and the lies we have believed and has woven them into our marriages. He knows that if we were to see the truth and submit to God's plan he would be defeated in yet another area of our lives. You see, Satan loses in the end and he knows it. However, he will steal our joy whenever he is allowed because that is his job.[39] The good news is that we are not helpless victims. In the end, because of Jesus, we win. In our daily lives, we *can* defeat him by submitting to God, asking for the power of the Holy Spirit, following the example of Jesus, and choosing to clear out the weeds. All we need to do is be willing to let go of being in control.

I know this may be more than you are able to take in all at once. Some of you are struggling so mightily in your marriages that it is hard for you to even look at your husbands. Some of you have even given up hope that things will ever work out. Others of you simply may be disillusioned and lost in confusion about what to do to help repair the damage. When we are operating from a place of hurt, it is extremely difficult to see how anything can ever change. I have been there, and so have hundreds of women just like you. Ask God for His help. Get straight with God about what's going on in your marriage, what your part has been (good and bad), and ask Him what He wants you to do in it to be the wife He created you to be. Meet with a Christ-centered counselor or your pastor and discuss the issues you are dealing with. Then, try to let go and let God lead (we will struggle with consistency here, but God's grace will cover all of it because He sees our heart's desire to try). The result may be a restored marriage, and it may not. What I can tell you, though, is that when you follow God He **will** work through the chaos for your good.[40]

Submission is a big concept loaded with all kinds of negative connotations. It can be tough to figure out just where to start. I have listed below some practical action steps you can use in this stage of the process. These have been cultivated through both my own experiences as well as those of the women I have taught over the years. This first step is based on an outflowing towards our husbands of the agape love we receive from God. We cannot do it in our own strength. I have learned that this requires a daily act of remembering that I am *choosing* to submit in order to be obedient to God. In truth, I have found this part to be both the most difficult and the most rewarding. Here are a few things I have tried:

1. Ask yourself the following questions: How do your daily activities reflect the value you place on your husband and your marriage? Do your husband and marriage come before everything else in your life, or after? Submission is about putting your husband before everything else besides your relationship with Jesus. How much time do you actually spend interacting with your husband as a wife, not as a parent? If anything else receives more of your attention and energy, commit to praying about how to rearrange your priorities.

2. Pray for your husband and your marriage every day. When you start your day asking God to help you follow Him, include asking Him for the strength and heart to submit to your husband as well. (Remember that 5-second prayers and whole hours are equally received by God.) Submission is not a part of our

natural selves, so this daily reminder that you are choosing to do so and need God's help in order to do it, will help you cultivate the habit easier. In praying for your husband, focusing on what he's going through will help you to understand better his responsibilities in leading your family.

3. Remember to communicate with your husband in decision making. Try not to let the enemy tempt you into fear here. Discussing options with your husband does not mean that you are a doormat or that your opinion is otherwise without value. Discussion means you share the truth about how you are feeling, why you are asking for what you need, and ask him what he thinks about it.

Respect

Our submission, out of agape love sustained by the power of the Holy Spirit living within us, can then produce a willingness to respect our husbands--the second step. While you may not see any reason to respect your husband right now, God does. When we ask Him to show us how to respect our husbands we are shown ways we may have never thought of before. Again, remember that you are not seeking to do this in your own strength. Ask the Holy Spirit to show you how to do this.

While I was still beginning this process, I realized my disrespect had erected a wall between my husband and me. At the beginning of this process, I came to realize through prayer and reflection that I needed to thank my husband for both

> "Women as a group tend not to view respect as something very important, but to men it is everything."

working hard at his job and earning an income which allowed me to stay home with our children. At that time, I was still reeling from being uprooted from a career I loved, being moved across the country because of his job, and forced to be a stay-at-home mom (a position I believed was *beneath* me). However, *out of respect for God*, I chose to be obedient to Him. The evening I shared my thankfulness and appreciation with my husband began awkwardly. Yet, before I could finish he had begun to cry. When I offered my gratitude, it came across as respect for him and what he did to provide for our family. As a result, he felt loved and a major piece of our barrier was destroyed.

Typically, as women, we take respect much more lightly than our husbands do. While we want to feel love first, and then we will offer respect; they want to feel respect first, and then they will offer love. Unfortunately, when we don't feel loved, we don't offer respect, and when they don't feel respected our husbands will withhold love. Thus, the vicious cycle continues. As with all disagreements in life, someone has to be the one to make a different choice. I believe God has called you to be that person. I have learned through experience that offering up a little respect has big rewards. After our conversation that night, we both began to change in very subtle, but very important ways. I continued to try and choose to be obedient to God's call to offer respect to my husband. In turn, God worked changes in him that I had been nagging my husband to do for years.

Women as a group tend not to view respect as something very important, but to men it is everything. If they don't feel respected, they are liable to react by holding themselves back from the person who is not giving them respect. It is part of who they are. As wives, it can be our *privilege* to offer our husbands respect as a way of helping them to feel confident and secure in who they are as men. We are singularly capable of helping our husbands in this way. (Remember that part in Genesis 2:18 about being a *"helper suitable?"*[41]) If you are feeling like your husband is lacking in his qualities as a man, offering him your respect is your opportunity to build him up. When your husband believes he is a capable, strong man he can then offer the love you desire. While this second step overlaps that of submission (when we submit, we are offering respect to our husbands), here are some additional activities I have used to show respect:

1. I have learned a great deal about my husband by reading. I have found it incredibly insightful to learn my husband's love language as well as his personality type. (I have used *The Five Love Languages* by Gary Chapman and *Personality Plus* by Florence Littauer for this.)

2. Set aside at least 10-15 minutes every day to spend time listening to your husband and sharing your day. Focus on using this time to really listen to your husband and what is going on with him. Turn your cell off. Ask the kids to leave you alone because you are spending time with your husband. Look your

husband in the eye and comment when appropriate. This may not go well at first, but what is important is your willingness to carve time out of your busy day just for your husband. If your husband is reluctant to set a specific time, or even commit to doing this at all, don't despair. Be on the lookout for other opportunities to show him you are putting him first, even if it is stopping whatever you are doing when he does speak to you in order to give him your full attention.

3. Get involved in what interests your husband. We continually want them to be involved and present with what we have going on in our lives, but when it is our turn we often become busy and uninterested. Showing interest in what's important to your husband will encourage him and help him to feel loved by you. When he feels loved, he will give it back.

Forgiveness

Learning to forgive our husbands for whatever grievances or hurts they may have caused in our marriages may be hard to even consider, but it can also be the most freeing thing we do. We do this not because they deserve it, but because we want to be obedient to God. We could never hope to be made right with God had we not received forgiveness through the shed blood of Jesus. We don't deserve to be forgiven for any sin we have ever committed in our lives. Yet we are, fully and without regret. How can we then deny the same forgiveness to our husbands who are merely human, born with a sinful nature that they must struggle against just as we do? Holding on to these grievances and past hurts is as harmful, if not more so, than any sinful act or behavior that occurred in our marriages. When we hold on to pain, we deny the healing power of Jesus to enter and restore us. It is also in direct opposition to God's Word that tells us to *"Bear with each other and forgive whatever grievances you may have against one another. Forgive as the Lord forgave you."* (Colossians 3:13)

I think all of us, when confronted with an apology and a request for forgiveness, feel compelled to accept that apology and give forgiveness. What is truly difficult is to feel healed of the hurt we received as a result of our spouse's actions and to not seek a punishment or judgment on our own. This is where God's presence in our lives is so important: we will fail if we try to forgive in our own power. Because we have been hurt, and have an absence of trust, we quite honestly may want the person who hurt us to pay for what they have done. How can we truly forgive without God's help under these circumstances?

Since marriage was designed by God to be an instrument of companionship and intimacy, the hurts we receive from our spouses can be much more painful. However, this does not excuse us from forgiveness. We were loved and forgiven before we were created because we have always been known by God[42] and because of this love, we are to love one another the same way and forgive others in return.[43] Is this hard? YES! Is this impossible despite whatever circumstances you are in? NO!

Forgiveness is often confused with freedom: we often believe that forgiving a person means they "got away" with whatever hurt they caused. This is not true. Focus on the Family in an article as part of their Forgiveness and

Restoration series, lists out what forgiveness is and is not like this:[44]

- Forgiveness is not letting the offender off the hook.

- Forgiveness is returning to God the right to take care of justice.

- Forgiveness is not letting the offense recur again and again.

- Forgiveness does not mean we have to revert to being the victim.

- Forgiveness is not the same as reconciling.

- Forgiveness is a process, not an event.

- We have to forgive every time.

- Forgetting does not mean denying reality or ignoring repeated offenses.

- Forgiveness is not based on others' actions but on our attitude.

- If they don't repent, we still have to forgive.

- We don't always have to tell them we have forgiven them.

- Withholding forgiveness is a refusal to let go of perceived power.

- (*specifically for divorce*) We might have to forgive more than the divorce. Post-divorce problems related to money, the kids, and schedules might result in the need to forgive again and to seek forgiveness ourselves.

- We might forgive too quickly to avoid pain or to manipulate the situation. We have to be careful not to simply cover our wounds and retard the healing process.

- We might be pressured into false forgiveness before we are ready.

- Forgiveness does not mean forgetting.

- Forgiveness starts with a mental decision.

When we choose to forgive, we are freeing two people from the pain of the event. First, we free ourselves from having to carry the burden of our pain using our own strength. Second, forgiveness frees the other person to be judged by God alone. When we withhold forgiveness, we actually stand in place of God's judgment on the other person, and even sometimes involve ourselves in it. I am not saying that we are so powerful as to be able to thwart God, but we can be used by the enemy. By harboring bitterness and resentment, we can divert the lesson and consequences God wants the other person to learn. The enemy can then twist our resentment and turn things that were meant by God to be good into something horrible, twisted, and ugly. This often results in additional bitterness and anger at the other person, which further prevents any real healing.

Overall, forgiveness is about YOU. It offers freedom from the repercussions of someone else's actions so that you can move forward instead of remaining chained to the situation and having bitterness, resentment, anger, fear and worry come into your heart and take over. It is hard but, because of Jesus, not impossible for us. Here are some of the ways to help you:

1. Holding on to our pain gets in the way of God's plans for our marriage. God wants us to have His perfect marriage, but He needs us to let go of the pain. Make a list of every hurt you are still bitter or resentful about. Then, one at a time, try to forgive your husband for each of them. This is a process that will need to be repeated over and over for a while until the pain subsides. (I still find myself needing to forgive my husband for things he did in the past.)

2. You may also find it helpful to talk things out with a trusted, mature Christian friend or pastor or Christ-centered counselor who can help you see how to work through your pain. Sometimes discussion can help us better understand exactly what we are dealing with.

3. Take time to express your emotions and allow healing to begin. So often we want to put the past behind us without ever dealing with any of the emotions surrounding it. If you are angry, be angry. If you are sad, be sad. If you are hurting, tend to your wounds. All our emotions are God-given and should not be pushed down. However, how we express them can be either God-centered or sinful-nature-centered. I have learned to regularly express my anger, frustration, sadness, and any other negative emotion in many ways. My favorite is boxing. Your mode may be painting, cleaning, running, or any number of things. The key is to choose something non-self-destructive.

Intimacy

Offering forgiveness allows us to move into the fourth step--building both emotional and physical intimacy. Emotional intimacy refers to the passion we feel as a result of being in love with our husbands. Physical intimacy refers to the physical union of a man and woman into one flesh. It is important to note that with submission to our husbands, our offer of respect, and our willingness to forgive, intimacy can develop. Without these three steps, trying to have intimacy would be like trying to build a house without a foundation, support beams, or framework.

For women, when there is no emotional intimacy, physical intimacy is very hard to develop. While for men, physical intimacy is a need they have that is not necessarily based on emotional intimacy whatsoever. Anything in our marriage that blocks the development of emotional intimacy makes it difficult for us as women to willingly offer physical intimacy. This offering of our bodies however, is another form of respect for our husbands. So, in response, when they do not feel we are physically available to them they may feel a lack of love. They may then withhold their emotional love for us, thus beginning again the negative cycle.

Since emotional intimacy is an important precursor to physical intimacy, seeking to develop it can help create a feeling of desire for our husbands. This starts with us and how we think about both ourselves and our husbands. Our thoughts (as we learned in Chapter Four) have a huge impact on our beliefs and our actions. If we think about ourselves or our husbands negatively, we have a much harder time even feeling like we want to create any kind of intimacy. One of the reasons why I wrote Chapter Four of this book was to help you receive freedom from the negative thoughts that might be controlling how you see yourself so that you can be free to receive the love Jesus offers. In the context of marriage, we can experience a greater level of intimacy with our husbands the more we begin to believe God's truth about us. When we do, our husband's attitudes towards us no longer determine our worth. When our husband's attitudes no longer determine our worth we are free to develop intimacy without fear.

Opening up to developing emotional intimacy can be scary. It requires change, vulnerability, and risk. In my own marriage developing emotional intimacy meant learning to meet my husband on his level instead of requiring him to always meet me on mine. I prefer to be outdoors exploring or doing something I believe to be constructive, like projects in our home or learning a new skill or helping others. My husband prefers to be much quieter, engaging in activities that are more often solitary.

While I have come to understand he is wired differently than I, and I have made peace with the fact that we approach life differently, finding common ground to connect emotionally has been difficult, but not impossible. At first I had to tend to the feelings of resentment that bubbled up: "Why do we always have to do what he wants?" I would often complain to God. But, true to His word, my willingness has been blessed. Again, we do not have a perfect marriage (because perfect marriages do not exist), but we do have a healthy marriage which, because of my willingness to trust God first, is bringing much more joy than there was before.

I do not know where the level of intimacy lies in your marriage. I do not know what you have tried or not tried. Developing intimacy in your marriage however is not something you can do without first offering your submission, respect, and forgiveness. These three actions alone help build a foundation of deeper emotional intimacy, which can lead to more satisfying physical intimacy. For women, we find it very difficult to be physically intimate without having an emotional connection. However, we must understand, and accept, that men have been hard-wired the other way around. They develop emotional intimacy as a result of physical intimacy. When we lean on God to help us cultivate intimacy in a way that is rewarding for both us and our husbands, we can have an opportunity for the relationship we long for. Here are the things that have worked the best for me:

1. A good place to start is with the book *The Five Love Languages* by Gary Chapman. I recommend the one written specifically for marriage, but the general version will work as well. This book helped me to see that how I was trying to love my husband was not how he received love, and vice versa. Once we realized this and learned each other's love language, we were able to show our love much more clearly to one another.

2. Spend some time remembering what you felt while you were dating your husband. Look at old photographs, read through an old diary or journal, and search your heart for forgotten memories of special times between the two of you.

3. Date your husband. This can be an elaborate dinner out, or it can simply be a late dinner or special dessert after the kids go to bed. It can even be watching a favorite sports team or TV show together without interruption from cell phones, kids, or anything else.

4. Take care of your physical body. As any woman will tell you, it is extremely difficult to want to be physically intimate when we are feeling horribly about our bodies. Take time to figure out what it is that makes you feel that way. Are you eating poorly? Are you sedentary most of the day? Could you benefit from taking time to update your overall appearance? Be careful here! God created you in His own image, and you ARE beautiful the way you are. Truthfully, most of our husbands wonder why we are so upset with ourselves. How we treat ourselves has lasting effects on our psyches, however. If you have been leaving yourself at the bottom of the barrel, it's time, for the sake of intimacy in your marriage, to put yourself back where you belong.

5. Spend time discovering each other's bodies. What actions, touches, caresses, scents, etc., increase your desire to be physically intimate? Does your husband know them? Do you know his? Do you use them?

6. Set aside time to develop a hobby or common interest that fits your budget and the season of life you are in at this time.

7. Set aside time for some long-term time away with each other. So many couples, especially those with

young children, neglect this special time. Again, it doesn't have to be complicated. Simply spending a whole day together in your hometown can be great if an overnight stay is not possible at this season of your life.

• • •

Please remember, all of the suggestions I have included in this chapter are only things meant to get you thinking about where God might be leading you in your marriage. I share what I know in the hopes that it will open you up to asking God to show you what He has planned for you, not so that you can compare or follow blindly what has worked for me. Cultivating peace in your marriage may look much different than what it has looked like in mine. The bottom line is that peace can be received in *all* of our marriages when we invite God to lead us in what that might look like.

Let's Pray

Father God, thank You for the gift of marriage. While it doesn't always feel like a gift, and is often filled with more hurt than we'd like, we are choosing to believe that with You, all things are possible. Thank You for guiding us in how to become the wives You created us to be. Please help us to trust You. Please give us wisdom and strength to make the changes You ask us to, and to stop comparing our marriages to others. We believe You are more than capable of restoring our marriages in accordance with Your will and entrust this most special relationship to You. Amen.

"God is our refuge and strength, an ever-present help in trouble."

Psalm 46:1 NIV

Chapter Six

Cultivating Peace within the Family

"But blessed is the one who trusts in Me alone; the Eternal will be his confidence. He is like a tree planted by water, sending out its roots beside the stream. It does not fear the heat or even drought. Its leaves stay green and its fruit is dependable, no matter what it faces."

Jeremiah 17:7-9 the VOICE

Six

I remember the day I discovered I was pregnant. I had woken up like usual and was getting ready when my husband sprayed the hairspray that he had used for forever and I completely gagged. The rest of the day I spent worrying over the thought that after only one month of trying, we were pregnant. I remember heading to the gym and checking out racquetball equipment and spending a whole hour beating that ball against the wall because I was so frustrated that we were pregnant already. You'd think I would have been happy, but I wasn't. My husband and I had planned on having a year to get ready for this because that's what my doctor had told us. My best girlfriend and I had planned on experiencing pregnancy together, but she had yet to become pregnant after over a year of trying. Nothing was going according to my plan and I was completely freaked out.

In preparation for our daughter's birth, I read the book <u>What to Expect when You're Expecting</u>. We decorated her nursery and washed and sorted all her new clothes. We interviewed in-home childcare opportunities and selected one close to where I worked. We toured our local hospital and I packed a bag. That was it. For most of the nine months I was pregnant I was in a state of emotional turmoil. I *wanted* to be excited I was pregnant. I *wanted* to be happy. But I wasn't. It felt as if my whole world was falling apart. My husband was struggling to accept he was going to be a father and, as a result, had shut down emotionally. My best friend still wasn't pregnant and couldn't handle being around me because I was. I knew no one else who was pregnant or who even had young children. I had no one to talk to.

At that time, I was working as a high school English teacher. Two weeks before my possible due-date approached my doctor recommended I begin my leave-of-absence, but I knew if I could make it just a little longer my 8 weeks of paid vacation time could be extended by an additional 10 days with Christmas break. Otherwise, I would have to have unpaid leave and I didn't believe we could afford for me to stay home if I was not still receiving a paycheck. My last day of work, because my doctor ordered it, was Friday, October 31. Our daughter was born the following Monday, November 3.

The Monday after our Christmas break, 10 weeks after giving birth, I returned to work. All my classes were before lunch, leaving my schedule open in the afternoon. So, in order to cut down on our child-care costs, we had sought and received my school administration's permission for me to leave early so that I could pick our daughter up and take her home at my lunch time. I would use that "free time" to grade and plan and have my evenings "free" to cook and clean. It seemed like the *perfect* plan at the time. Reality, however, was far from perfect. Due to the new pressures of fatherhood and several other issues in his life, my husband began to suffer from depression and further withdrew. Grading and planning took much longer than I had anticipated. Our daughter was needier and much more active than I had envisioned as well.

The first three years of my daughter's life are a complete blur. Our daughter didn't sleep through the night until after she turned one. She was needy and refused to be calmed by anyone other than me. The night we tried to let her "cry it out" so she would go to sleep on her own resulted in over three hours of screaming. She began walking at nine months and was running, always *away* from me, by 11 months. Once she could walk her stroller and car seat became her enemy and she could only be physically forced into either. She was fierce... something we would later realize was termed "strong-willed," and she ran the show in every way imaginable.

There were moments of joy and fun between the madness. She loved to dance. When she was little we would bounce all around the living room. After she could walk she discovered Shania Twain and would "perform" for me. She liked to make cookies with me, sitting on the counter to pour in the chocolate chips. She was curious about everything, often digging in the dirt or following a ladybug, or picking up snails to check underneath. She loved to dress up and play make-believe. The only time she was still was when I would read to her or when she was watching a movie (Disney movies are still her favorite to this day) and so we read a lot and had a full video library. She brought life into every room she entered... even if that life looked like a whirlwind.

> "I believed I was a complete failure as a mom because I couldn't get my daughter to do anything other than what she wanted."

Trying to grade and plan while caring for our daughter, our home, and everything else during those three years completely overwhelmed me. I believed I was a complete failure as a mom because I couldn't get my daughter to do anything other than what she wanted. I couldn't get my husband to help out either so I also believed I was a failure as a wife. I couldn't keep my house clean, I rarely knew what I was making for dinner (and when I did I never had all the ingredients I needed), and the laundry seemed to never end...all more reasons to believe I was doing it all wrong. Then my performance at work began to suffer, further adding to the shame I felt.

I was a complete mess, but no one knew. To the outside world, I was organized, competent, accomplished, there for them, and ready to take on whatever challenge or need anyone else had. At home, though, I screamed, yelled, manipulated, and raged. My marriage began to unravel. My daughter increasingly acted out. I began to hate my job, the one thing I had always wanted to do and had always loved. There was no peace in my life, only exhaustion. What I didn't realize at the time was that I was trying to live a perfect life instead of a grace-filled one.

• • •

Parenting is tough. If you are already a parent you know it is one of the most difficult of all our relationships to nurture. Creating any form of sustainable peace within it often seems impossible. Our children's unruly emotions and undisciplined natures often clash with our own insecurities and anxieties creating a haven for trouble. When you combine the personalities and needs of one or more children and the personalities and needs of one or both parents, trying to create a peace-filled family environment has the potential to be completely over-whelming, *but it can be done.* While my initial parenting journey was filled with chaos, because of God's love, grace, healing, and mercy it has not stayed that way.

The process of learning to receive God's peace in the middle of a chaotic family situation begins with this fact: abuse within a family requires professional help. As I mentioned in the chapter on Cultivating Peace in Marriage, if abuse is present, please stop reading right now and consider calling the National Domestic Abuse Hotline at 1-800-799- SAFE (7233) or www. thehotline.org. I am in no way qualified to help you navigate through the struggles of such a family relationship.

Keeping in mind our gardening metaphor, think of cultivating peace in our families as allowing God to teach us how to nurture the seed He planted when He added our children. Just as we needed to have Him teach us how to nurture the seed of our role as a wife, we need Him to teach us how to be the mothers our children need. There are new promises from God's nourishing Word we can claim. There will be weeds to clear out. We will need to soak in the Light of Jesus, prune activities and relationships with the wisdom of the Holy Spirit, and tend to this seed with God's love, grace and mercy. Our willingness to remain connected to Him will directly impact the development of the fruit of this precious relationship.

Before we dig into how to receive God's peace in our relationships with our children and families, I want to remind you of something. No matter how old your children are at this

> "Without Jesus there is no lasting peace, not just within ourselves and our marriages, but also within the relationships we have with our own children."

moment, no matter how filled with chaos your relationships are, they are not beyond God's love, grace, healing, and mercy. Whatever mistakes you believe you have made as a mom, they can be forgiven. Whatever regrets you have, God can use them for good. No matter how far apart you are, with God nothing is impossible. God's word is infallible. And, *I am proof.* God has used *all* the chaos of my early parenting years for good—my good, my children's good, my husband's good (and the good of our marriage and family), and now hopefully your good. *I do not have it all figured out*; I don't believe any of us ever will until we are in heaven, but maybe my mistakes and the redemption Jesus has provided can offer you hope and fill you with the courage to try His way over your own.

Cultivating the peace we are looking for in our families starts with us. That is why it is so important to have a relationship with Jesus. Without Jesus, there is no *lasting* peace, not just within ourselves and our marriages, but also within the relationships we have with our own children. He alone offers the pathway to God's wisdom, forgiveness, grace, and freedom.

Additionally, I believe God created the family unit to grow us closer to Him no matter what form it takes. Today's families may be shaped by two biological parents, a single parent, step-parents, grandparents as parents, and adoptive parents. Yet the many differing models of families are all important to God and equally in need of Divine help through life's many challenges. Each person within a family, whether biological or not, was placed there by God for the purpose of being refined into the person God created them to become. Weaknesses and strengths are magnified in a family so that they can be developed and nourished. The role then of a parent within the family is to be a leader in this process for their children. This is why God began with *me*, and why I began this book with *you*. As we understand why we need God, we begin to model that need for our children.

This chapter is divided into two different parts: Parenting and Family. It's important to note here that when I mention "family" in this chapter, I am referring to the adults and children most directly associated with each other. What I am *not* referring to is the inclusion of extended family members (either related by blood or marriage) who are not directly involved in the day-to-day activities and responsibilities of parenting.

Parenting

When I was in the infant stages of my role as a parent I had no idea what I was doing. This in itself is part of being a new parent, but I was dangerous because I *believed* I could be in complete control... until God sent me a very strong-willed daughter who ran right through me and over me all day every day. I grew angrier and angrier the more I felt like things weren't turning out the way they were *supposed* to. I began frantically trying in vain to grasp control over anything I could--my job, my home, my marriage, you name it! Chaos reigned; any small blessings of peace were quickly destroyed.

> "I continued to struggle for years because... I wanted God to work things out the way I thought they were supposed to work."

Not until I suffered the miscarriage of our second child did I realize how bad things had become. Six months later, when I rejoiced over the news that I was pregnant with our son, I made the decision that things had to change. I couldn't ignore the chaos anymore and so I chose to believe in the truth of Jesus and asked Him for His peace.

I wish I could say that things got better immediately after inviting Jesus into my heart, but they didn't. I continued to struggle for years because, as I shared earlier, I wanted God to work things out the way I thought they were supposed to work out rather than submitting to His will. I have learned much over the years as I slowly let go of being in control of what my role as a parent was *supposed* to look like, and instead chose to trust God's view, but it took a while and I am still learning.

Accepting Jesus' free gift of salvation opens up direct access to God, who in return forgives us and grants us access to the power of the Holy Spirit. *Nothing then can stop us from becoming the parent God wants us to be for the children He has given to us.* There is no hectic schedule in the world that is so set in stone that God cannot redesign it. There is no insecurity so profound that God cannot strengthen it. There is no child whom God cannot speak to in a way they will hear. All God wants is for us to invite Him to work *through* us in our role as parents.

Carrying out our role as parents according to our own understanding of the best way of doing so is what creates the majority of the chaos we experience. Cultivating peace in our parenting begins when we step back and invite Him in to lead us in becoming the mother our children need us to be. We can navigate this change by using the same steps as we did for ourselves and our relationship with Jesus, only appropriate for our children: 1) *submit* to God's plan for their lives; 2) *respect* each of our children as individual human beings with separate interests and ideas; 3) *forgive* them when they cause us grief; and 4) build *intimacy* with them on their level so they are comfortable coming to us for guidance.

Allowing God to direct my steps as a parent has brought much-needed relief to me, my marriage, our children, and our family as a whole. While I do not claim perfection in any of these areas, I have come to understand their importance for our children and my ever-changing role as their mother. Especially as they have gotten older I have realized how freeing and valuable it is to choose to invite God to parent them through me, rather than fighting to parent them in my own strength.

Submission

In the role of cultivating peace as a parent, submission comes in two forms: Submitting to God's plan for us as parents of the children we have been given and, if present, submission to our husbands as the leaders of the family. As with all other areas, submission to God comes from admitting that we cannot fulfill our responsibilities as a parent without His help. Submitting to our husbands can often be more difficult than submitting to God because things like trust, respect, and a belief that we as mothers know the best way to raise our children often get in the way of allowing our husbands to lead. As with our marriages, whether or not your husband is walking with God is not a determiner of his ability to lead the family. God will work through your husband, but you have to trust that He will.

If you are a single parent, for whatever reason, God is gracious and promises to step in and fill the role of *"A father to the fatherless, a defender of widows, is God in his holy dwelling."* (Psalm 68:5 NIV) You have the Most High God as the Father of your children!

If you are a step-parent, parenting can at times seem overwhelmingly complicated due to custody agreements and the emotional scars of divorce. Know that God is still with you, especially in the complications, and that He knows your circumstances. His peace *is* available in the middle of whatever chaos your circumstance is producing at this moment.[45] No matter your parenting circumstance, submission to God as a way of receiving His peace in a chaotic parenting situation centers on believing that He can, and will, guide you in how to most effectively parent the children He has given you.

Most of the chaos we may experience as parents comes from trying to parent in our own strength and understanding of how things *should* be. He knows our children as well as He knows us. He uniquely created each one of them and wrote all the days of their lives "before one of them came to be," just as He did for us.[46] Submitting to His will allows for us to lay down false expectations and impossible standards in favor of living in the freedom of watching Him work through us. When we no longer strive to achieve, we are released to simply be a parent moment by moment, experiencing the joys and learning from the lessons that come. *That's* how we learn to receive God's peace within our families.

We have been given the gift of nurturing another life, and it is an incredible responsibility, but not one that we shoulder on our own. Submission to God's will allows Him to mold us into the mama he created us to be for the children He planned to give us from before we were born. It is not easy to let go, I know, but it has been incredible to see how powerful God's peace has been in response to *my* obedience. Notice that I refer to the changes as being in response to my obedience. We cannot change our husbands or our parenting situation, but when we choose to follow God, He can work amazing changes that we could never have anticipated or created in our own strength.

Here are some things in the area of submission in parenting to consider:

1. Pray daily for your children and your role as a parent. Are you struggling with fear, uncertainty, worry, or any thing else related to your children? Pray for them. Pray with them. I have found it helpful to be a part of a parent's prayer group. One I enjoyed was Mom's In Prayer International (www.momsinprayer org).

2. Read about Christ-centered parenting or join a group that is learning how to parent through their relationship with Jesus. There are many resources available, but one I have used personally is <u>Growing Kids God's Way</u> by Gary and Marie Ezzo of Growing Families USA (www.growingfamiliesusa.com).

3. Have conversations with your husband/children's father about parenting issues. I have learned that when parents are on the same page in all major decisions affecting their children, they have a greater ability to stand firm in their resolve to stick to the decisions they make. When children realize they cannot "divide and conquer," they are more likely to comply.

4. Allow your husband/children's father to parent his way (barring abusive, neglectful or otherwise harmful behaviors). The same rules and decisions can be handled differently, *yet just as effectively*, by each parent. Trial and error are part of parenting for both parents. Because of Jesus we can receive forgiveness and grace when we mess up, and He asks us to extend the same to others in our lives as well.

Respect

Our children were created in God's image, just as we have been, and that alone is reason enough to offer them our respect. This *does not* mean that we treat them as our equals, but it *does* mean that we need to allow them to develop into the person God created them to be whether or not it looks like who *we* want them to be. Our style of discipline, the instruction we give, and the freedoms we allow our children to have needs to be based upon a genuine desire to reveal the awesome person God created each of our children to be. Respect for each of our children as uniquely created individuals with their own strengths, weakness, gifts, and talents further cultivates peace within our families because there is no longer a struggle to make them into something. We are free then to experience them just as they are and free to trust that God will give us whatever we need to parent them well.

There will still be those moments where what we know to be good for them clashes with their own ideas. That tension, I have found, is a part of the process our children must go through in order to own who they are. How we respond to those challenges makes all the difference. When my children were little, I learned that challenges were best managed with parent-centered consequences of time-outs, removal of privileges and groundings, coupled with explanations of why they were in trouble. As they have matured (they are 18 and 13 at the time of this publication), I have learned that challenges are more about them trying to figure out who they are and so there have been much fewer consequences from me, and more "natural consequences" (those consequences that are naturally a part of their choices, like getting a speeding ticket or a failing test grade). When those occur my role shifts to coaching them through the lesson they may need to learn.

While parenting with respect can be challenging, when we pray for guidance, we will be given the knowledge to parent in a way that's most effective for each of our children. I have found the following activities helpful in showing respect to my children:

1. Parent each child according to who they are. Take the time to really get to know your child. What is her love language? What is his personality type? What motivates her? What are his fears? What are her hopes

and dreams? Remember, these do not have to correspond with yours in order to be acceptable. Your children are individuals and when you allow them to explore who they are with unconditional acceptance from you, they feel respected. This action is an example of how we can teach the ways of the Lord to our children. Jesus loves everyone regardless of their mistakes, hang-ups, or improprieties. He knows each of us and meets us where we are. He leads the way to God by example, by showing us how much the Father loves us, and by telling us how to be strengthened by God. Parenting each child according to who they are, offers an opportunity for us as parents to reinforce the lessons of Jesus.

2. Watch and Listen. Observe and listen to your children as they interact with you, other adults, and other children. This is one of the best ways to learn about your children and see where to move next in your parenting journey. Are they struggling with bossy behavior? You can gently teach them about Jesus' servant heart. Are they fear-filled? You can share with them the stories of faith and strength in the Bible. You don't have to be a theologian, only willing to do a little research in your Bible or online for stories of servanthood, faith, strength, or any other issue your children are facing.

3. Learn to discipline with respect, not out of anger or fear. This is hard to do, but a necessary step to developing respect within our relationships with each

child. This takes self-control on our part not to blow up when a mistake or error of judgment occurs. I have seen that when I remain calm, so much more is accomplished in the name of peace. When I remember that my goal in discipline is not to punish but to impart wisdom and offer a chance to learn from the situation, there is peace in the disciplining on both my part and my child's. While disciplining with respect takes more patience and time, our children learn God's way of dealing with mistakes. This produces a willingness on their part to take more personal responsibility for their actions. As a result, we do not argue with them nearly as much as we used to and we are able to show our children through our actions a respectful, God-centered way to deal with the conflicts that arise.

4. Examine the expectations you have on your children: are they yours or God's? God designed your children for a specific purpose only they can fulfill. Are your actions as a parent showing respect for who God created them to be?

Forgiveness

Our children have a sinful nature, just like we do. They can cause all kinds of difficulties for us. Their behaviors, words, and overall reactions to us can often hurt us, frustrate us, and cause us to lose our tempers. In this, they are no different than any other human being, which is why we have to be intentional about forgiving them. *Just as we had to learn to receive forgive-*

ness for ourselves and learn to forgive our husbands, we also have to learn to forgive our children.

From infantile dependency that causes a rift in our marriage, to full-blown rebellion by a teenager, our resentment towards our children can be used by the enemy to cause all kinds of problems. My resentment towards my daughter remained for several years after that initial three-year-blur. It affected everything about our relationship; I had a very hard time loving her and there were times I did not like her at all. Allowing God to lead me through forgiving her for being born when she was, for being so strong-willed, for making me feel all kinds of insecurities because I couldn't control her, freed me from that hardness in my heart. I realized it was my reactions to her behavior that were sinful, not her. Once I sought forgiveness from God for my reactions and asked my daughter for her forgiveness (a practice I use regularly in my messy parenting journey), peace between us began to grow.

A lack of forgiveness on our part as well can prevent our children from learning how to offer it to others. One of the main responsibilities we have as parents is to model the love of Jesus for them. If He forgives us, but we do not forgive them, we can potentially create a disconnect from that authentic love that our children need as much as we do. Forgiveness then is not only a way to cultivate peace within our relationships with our children but also a way to teach them the ways of God. Here is what I have learned about forgiveness and letting go:

1. Accept that your child(ren) have a sinful nature that is strong because they have not developed the dependency upon the power of the Holy Spirit to combat

it. I do not advocate dismissing negative behavior as "boys/girls will be boys/girls" but I do believe that our reactions need to be tempered to their maturity level. Negative behavior moments can then become great teachable times in which we show them how their behavior affected us, support the consequence (whether it's a natural or parent-given one) with Scripture, and allow them to try again. Life is a process of learning through consequences and blessings (again, both natural and parent-given) how to follow God. Our forgiveness of their mistakes allows them to heal and grow.

2. If you realize you are holding on to resentment or bitterness as a result of your child's actions, search your heart for a way to repent and receive forgiveness. Start by praying to God about how you are feeling and the situation that caused it. Then, if you are prompted to do so, verbally offer forgiveness to your child. I have done this and the result has been amazing both for my children and me. I was able to let go and allow peace back into my heart which restored our relationship, and my children have been able to see a model of forgiveness first-hand.

3. When your child does something wrong, teach them to do more than say "I'm sorry." We have taught our children to say specifically what they are sorry for and then ask for forgiveness from the person they hurt. We taught them this through modeling it ourselves. I tell them specifically what I am sorry for doing and

ask them if they will forgive me. This has taught them that we all are the same when it comes to messing up and that we all need to repair the situation through forgiveness, just as God commands us to do. (Colossians 3:13)

Intimacy

Building intimacy with our children is more than just spending time with them. It involves learning to marvel and delight at who they are right now, in spite of the difficulties we encounter as parents. When we learn to respect that they are individuals, and forgive them for their mistakes in judgment, we involve ourselves in building an actual relationship with them. Setting aside time to develop this area is based on the quality of the time we have with our children, not the quantity.

Working outside of the home does not keep you from being able to build authentic relationships with your children, any more than working in the home makes it easier. Parenting is tough, no matter the circumstances you face; that's why we need God. When we receive peace in our personal relationship with God through a personal relationship with Jesus Christ we begin to learn the importance of building relationships. That sense of connectedness pours out of us, creating a longing to build other authentic relationships with the others in our lives, from our husbands (if present) to our children. God knows our circumstances, He knows our time constraints; He will make sure to use the time we have to the best of His ability to create lasting connections with our kids. All He needs from us is a willing heart to invite Him in to do so.

Building intimacy is dependent upon *how* we spend the time we have with our children, no matter how short it may be. It's about being present, trusting that God will take care of everything else as we seek to develop the relationships in our lives over taking care of the things. Our children do need us in their lives, infancy through adulthood; it just looks different in each season. When they are little, building intimacy may be all about entering their world and engaging with them in it. As they grow, intimacy may look like giving them space to work through the situations they face, but remaining available to be a sounding board. As my parenting journey continues I often find myself using multiple ways to build intimacy with each of my children, some of which work and some of which fall flat. The key is to keep trying and not let discouragement steal the fact that God knows your heart and He is working on your behalf, even when it seems like your child may never want to build any kind of relationship with you.

"God knows our circumstances, He knows our time constraints; He will make sure to use the time we have to the best of His ability to create lasting connections with our kids.

While my activities are ever-changing, here are some of the ways I have been able to consistently build intimacy with my children.

1. Date your children individually. Spend time one-on-one with each child as often as you can, and make your time together all about them. This doesn't have to be fancy, but remember what works for one child may not work for another. If at first you are met with resistance, do not give up. Teenagers especially will push away to see if you are really sincere in your efforts to be with them. Keep asking to spend time with them, but don't force them to. Trust God that He will provide the opportunities as long as you are willing.

2. Be involved with what's going on in their lives. If you have a child who loves Lego's, learn all you can about them. If you have a child who loves a certain book series, read the series too. Listen to their music. Pay attention to their friends. Play with them. When we seek to live at the level of our children once in a while, we develop a relationship with them based on who they are, not on who we want or need them to be.

3. Tell your children stories about you. When they are struggling, offer to tell them a time when you struggled too. When they are having friendship issues, tell them your friendship issues. When they have made a mistake, tell them your mistakes too. Tell them the silly, embarrassing stuff. Tell them the sad stuff. Let them see you as a six-year-old, a pre-teen, teenager, or a young mother. Intimacy is a two-way street. If you want to build a lasting relationship with your children, they have to know who you

are too. An additional benefit is that this activity can be used to teach the ways of the Lord to our children. When Jesus wanted to teach about the character of God, did. He make a big deal of it? Did He require all kinds of stuff to be done? No. He spoke in parables in order to relate God's Word to their very real lives. You can do that! Your life is full of stories you can use to illustrate the Word through basic concepts like obedience, faith, trust, and consequences.

We begin to cultivate peace in our relationships with our kids through 1) modeling submission to God in parenting, 2) respecting them based on God's plan for their life, 3) offering forgiveness when they hurt us or cause us pain and, 4) building intimacy through sharing quality time together. The ideas I have included here are simply a few things we can do as parents to nurture the seed of peace within our relationship with our children. The good news is that you are not shouldering the weight of this responsibility on your own: You have the divine power of the entire Trinity (God the Father, God the Son (Jesus) and God the Spirit (Holy Spirit)) to guide, nurture and work on *your* behalf. You *can* receive peace in the chaos of your relationships with your children. God placed you as their mama for a reason, and He who called you is faithful to complete and equip you.

> *"Now may the God of peace, who through the blood*
> *of the eternal covenant brought back from the dead our*
> *Lord Jesus, that great Shepherd of the sheep, equip you with*
> *everything good for doing his will, and may he work in us*
> *what is pleasing to him, through Jesus Christ, to whom be*
> *glory for ever and ever. Amen."*

(Hebrews 13:20-21 NIV)

• • •

Family

The word *family* can cause many different reactions within us. Our family of origin may have been a source of peace or one of chaos or somewhere in between. Our current family may be filled with hurt, trauma (such as from the death of a parent or abuse), division, and chaos, or it may not. I think you will agree that *family* is a word loaded with feelings. No matter our family circumstance, however, choosing to follow God's plan can cultivate the peace we long for in ways we could never have imagined.

Several years ago, if you had asked me to describe my family situation I would have said "chaotic." My husband and I did not engage in healthy communication, and as a result often parented our children at opposite ends of the spectrum. He was very lenient and indulgent. I took my stance at the opposite extreme. It was a battle and our children were in the middle. My own personal chaos affected my role as a parent as well. Often insecure and definitely living life through my weeds, I was not a very consistent parent.

My children were constantly in a state of confusion as they never really knew which mommy would greet them today: Complacent Mommy? Happy Mommy? Angry Mommy? Overwhelmed Mommy? Sometimes they would get multiple mommies in one day. Needless to say, spending time as a family was not something I wanted to do. However, I couldn't deny I had a longing for a close, loving family. I didn't know how to get from where I was to where my heart longed to be, though. Looking at my current circumstances, the chaos I was living in, it seemed impossible that any dream of a healthy family could ever be realized. It was often a prayer of mine to ask God to heal my family, to help me be the parent He wanted me to be, and to guide me in creating the family I longed for.

I have been told to be careful what you pray for. I never could have guessed how God would answer my prayer for a closer family. Incredibly, when our family was in its most difficult stage, God called us into homeschooling. We had some awful days, but God's plan was to use this forced twenty-four-hour togetherness to weed out lies, to strip me of my expectations, and to tear down our family to its foundations... much like the process He used within me personally. Then He built us up, little by little, as individuals and as a unit. The four-and-a-half years we spent as a full-time homeschooling family were some of the roughest times for us, but our common struggle brought us closer together than we ever could have become on our own.

I am not advocating that you drop everything and become a homeschooling family, or even that homeschooling is the best way to develop a close family. What I am trying to show you is that when you follow God's plan, *even if it*

> "What I am trying to show you is that when you follow God's plan, even if it makes no sense to you, He rewards your obedience in ways you could never have imagined."

makes no sense to you, He rewards your obedience in ways you could never have imagined. Today I would tell you my family is quite "normal," with a smile. We have our regular conflicts and busy schedules. However, I will also tell you that my teenage daughter and I have an amazing relationship... yes, that same daughter whom I fought with so much when she was a little girl. I will also tell you that I have been able to watch God work changes in my children that as a parent I struggled to accomplish. My husband and I are also now on the same page in our parenting. No more battle with our children in the middle. How did we get here? I chose to follow God's design for my family. Please don't think for a minute that I am boasting. I did nothing to achieve this, and I certainly don't believe I ever deserved it. I chose to follow God. *He* did the rest.

I do not know what your family situation looks like today. I do not know the struggles you face or the hurts you have experienced or the trauma you have endured. I do not know what your expectations are or your hopes and dreams. I do know, however, that as long as we focus on how impossible things look to us, we are not able to see how powerful our God is. Nothing is impossible for Him. No situation is beyond His power to cultivate His peace. He can be trusted.

Will you choose to invite Him to step in, and allow Him to take the lead?

The process of learning to receive God's peace in the middle of your chaotic family situation (barring any abusive situation, as I mentioned at the beginning of this chapter) doesn't change simply because we are focusing on group rather than individual relationships. As we begin the process of cultivating peace within our marriages and the relationships we have with our children, it then becomes easier to cultivate peace within our family as a whole. Cultivating peace within a family, no matter what your family looks like, involves the same process we have been focusing on for all our relationships.

It starts with choosing to submit to God's plan for our families, and continues in choosing to respect our family enough to make it a priority within our lives, choosing to try and forgive the inconveniences and hurts that come from being a part of a family, and choosing to develop intimacy within our families whether or not they measure up to our expectations. When we intentionally choose to follow God's direction in developing our family in order to cultivate peace, we are also given the opportunity to teach our children how to deal with conflict, offer forgiveness, grant grace, lead others effectively, and so much more.

Many of the suggestions and commentaries about this process that I included in the previous part of this chapter can be used for the family as a whole, but here are some additional descriptors and activities that might be helpful.

Submission

The process of cultivating peace within our families starts with submission to God's leadership of our family, especially since today's family can have so many varied scenarios. No matter what your family looks like, God is capable of leading it. In His strength alone we can choose to receive Christ-centered wisdom for moving ahead from where you are right now, one step at a time. You may have a husband, or you may not. Your children may live with you, and they may not. Things may be complicated and you may be completely overwhelmed. No matter what your circumstance though, God has a way for you to experience His peace if you will choose to follow Him and His leadership of your family. You can choose to let go of trying to handle it all on your own and ask Him to step in instead.

1. Pray. Pray for peace, guidance, and healing within your family. Pray about what God had in mind when he created your family.

2. If you are married, remember to discuss any family ideas you have with your husband first. Then pray about them before you commit.

3. While God commands us to *"honor your father and mother so that you may live long in the land the Lord your God is giving you"* (Exodus 20:12), it also says that *"for this reason a man will leave his father and mother and be united to his wife, and they will become one flesh."* (Genesis 2:24) We offer submission when we choose to follow God and our

husbands' direction over our parents' opinions on how to run our families. The decision to create our own families can create friction for many of us. I have read the book <u>Boundaries</u> by Drs. Henry Cloud and John Townsend which has helped me learn how to respectfully submit to my husband without being disrespectful to my parents.

4. In a blended or single-parent family, submission can also mean honoring the divorce and custody agreements in place. This may be tough, especially if you don't agree with the decisions. Please know there is biblical precedent for submitting to the authority of governing bodies. Romans 13:1 says; *"Let everyone be subject to the governing authorities, for there is no authority except that which God has established. The authorities that exist have been established by God."* If you are struggling, use the proper channels to dispute the agreements, and invite God to be your champion for justice.

Respect

Too often the needs of our families get shoved to the bottom of the priority list. The daily demands of work, school and individual activity schedules, home care, and maintaining other relationships can leave the family unit as a whole hard-pressed to even find time to be together. Learning to develop respect within our family means that we make time for everyone to be together. This takes time and intentionally watching for where God is leading. Try not to rush anything and certainly don't get discouraged if your first efforts are unsuccessful. Remember, this is a process.

1. If you are married, ask your husband if he is willing to try praying with you about how to develop respect within your family. Spend time both together and separately praying about the season your family is in, your children's personalities, and the amount of time you have to devote to family activities. Then talk together about where you feel God is leading you and try to follow Him. If you have a husband who will not pray (either with you or on his own) don't worry. God is still in control and will hear your prayers for wisdom and guidance.

2. If you are not married, spend time with God in prayer about the season your family is in, your children's personalities and the amount of time you have to devote to family activities. Then commit to trying to follow God's lead.

3. Build respect based on your family today, not on your experience within the family of your past. Our family will be different from the family we grew up in, which means we need to leave behind any expectations about what our family should look like based on that model. When God steps in, everything changes. However, if we are seeing things through the past, we often miss the growth He is doing.

4. Make time for family activities. A family that prays, plays, works, and shares life together stays together

when the storms come. Consider setting a regular family time for activities where you serve together, play together, take care of your home together, or simply spend time with one another. It doesn't have to be the same time every week and can reflect the changing seasons your family will go through. Remember, the goal is to follow where God is leading.

Forgiveness

Forgiveness within a family can be tough not only because situations may be harsh, but because of the number of people involved. Often family squabbles move beyond the nuclear family into the extended family, involving in-laws and other relatives. If you have had situations where resentment and bitterness have developed, entering into the process of learning to forgive as well as repentance and asking for forgiveness can go a long way towards cultivating peace within your family. Here are some strategies to consider.

1. Pour the whole situation out to God. No matter how deep the hurt or how long ago it happened, God can and will heal you, when you ask Him to, on His timetable. He will also show you if you had any responsibility in the situation. If you do, repent and ask forgiveness. Then ask God if you should ask forgiveness within your family for your part in the situation, and submit to His authority if you feel you are being asked to do so.

2. Pray for those who have hurt you. Pray for them to see how they cause pain. Pray for strength to follow the ways of Christ when you interact. Allow God to use your obedience to Him as a catalyst for change in how you relate to anyone you may need to forgive.

3. Offer forgiveness to those who have hurt you. Every family has situations where someone gets hurt. You can either hold on to your hurts or you can let them go by forgiving the person who caused you pain. No parent, sibling, child, or other relative is outside of God's love, nor are they too far gone to be forgiven by the blood of Jesus. As followers of Christ, we are asked to offer that forgiveness, remembering that we too are sinners and have been forgiven.

4. Enter into community with other Christ-centered families. No family is without trouble and hearing how others struggle can help restore our hope that God is with us as well. Parenting, marriage, and relationships with our children can all overwhelm us at times, but opening up in a safe environment where the goal is to point each other back to Jesus (not fix each other) can help.

Intimacy

If you have been working through the activities of the first three parts of the process, you will have been simultaneously developing intimacy within your family. The process of creating intimacy also cultivates a sense of identity for those within your family. As intimacy increases, members are often seen as parts of the family, rather than individuals within it. Here are a few extra activities to help build intimacy.

1. Create a family mission statement. What does it mean to be a member of the "your family name here" family? Determine, with guidance from God (and your husband if present), the type of family you are in this season, and how you want to grow as a family. Are you a family that likes/needs to stay close to home or one that travels? Are you driven by helping others in your community? Do you like to organize neighborhood get-togethers? What does your family do well together right now? Once you have determined some areas of engagement, set aside time to develop them together.

2. Consider having regular family meetings. Set aside time to sit and talk about the family as a whole. Are there issues between siblings that need to be resolved? Do you have individual crises that need prayer? What plans can be made for the upcoming weeks and months?

3. Create a family calendar. List out who needs to do what and when so that it becomes easier to see where shared times to get together might be present. It can also be a huge eye opener to just how busy our daily lives are and a place to start praying about what God may want to prune. (I share a great tool for this, the Schedule Tracker™, on my website,

StephanieHaynes.net in the Digging Deeper link, under the Cultivating Peace tab.)

4. Develop a shared family activity. Do you like camping? Skiing? Bike riding? Sports? Even rotating through the top favorites when considering how to spend time together can be a way todevelop intimacy.

5. Try to just be together. All activities aside, the simplest moments are often the sweetest.

I know this is a lot to take in. Breathe. Remember this is a process that will take time. While that may make you more frustrated (you may want peace in your family NOW!), God does have a plan that can be trusted. Choosing to enter into this process with Him is the first step. You may have to start small and incorporate time with your family on a regular basis first before you can progress towards private time with each child. You may need to spend time changing your children's behaviors and your own. There may be tough decisions to make regarding your current schedule if it doesn't allow for you, your husband, and your children to be together. Rest assured though, no matter how chaotic you may feel, if you choose to invite God into your family situation, He will cultivate peace within it. Trust that He will show you the way.

Let's Pray

Father God, thank You for the families you have blessed us with. It may not be the family of our dreams and is often more chaotic than we'd like, but we are choosing to believe that You are bigger than all of that and that Your plans for our families surpass anything we could ever ask for or imagine. Please guide us in Your will for our families. Help us to follow You and help us to trust You over our own fears and worries. And, please help our whole family receive the peace You have to offer us. In Jesus' name, Amen.

"Know this: children are a gift from the Eternal;
the fruit of the womb is His reward.
Your sons born in your youth are a protection,
like arrows in the hand of a warrior.
Happy is the man who has his quiver full,
for they will help and protect him when he is old.
He will not be humiliated when he is accused at the gate,
for his sons will stand with him against his enemies."

Psalm 127:3-5, the VOICE

Chapter Seven

Cultivating Peace at Home

"Better a dry crust eaten in peace than
a house filled with feasting—and conflict"

Proverbs 17:1 NLT

Seven

When my life was its most chaotic, relationships were the furthest down on my priority list. Do you know what was near the top? Second only to my job (remember, that was where I used to find my identity), was my home: if it was clean and neat and organized I was happy. If it wasn't, look out! I lived under the idea that at any moment someone might come over and if my house was a mess that would mean I was somehow a failure.

I would completely freak out at the thought of all the preparations I believed needed to be made in order to entertain in our home. The house had to be spotless (even the areas no one would see), new decorative additions needed to be purchased (we *needed* new centerpieces and serving dishes), and the menu had to be incredible (no one wants regular old food do they?). Afterward when friends would offer to help clean up, I would cheerfully exclaim that I had it covered, only to spend half the night doing so on my own, growing more and more frustrated at all the work I had to do. My behaviors were so frustrating that my husband stopped wanting to have anyone over.

Day-to-day was just as bad. I couldn't tolerate any laundry build up, or dust, or dishes in the sink. I couldn't

> "I had fully bought into the lie that I only could be found acceptable to others if my home was without fault."

deal with weeds growing in our front yard, or an overgrown lawn, or an imperfect landscape. Toys were never to be left out, books and magazines were to a ways be neatly stacked, and closets were to be organized at all times. Yes, I was THAT woman. On the outside, it looked as if I was pulling it off flawlessly, but inside I was a fear-filled, stressed-out mess. I had fully bought into the lie that I only could be found acceptable to others if my home was without fault.

Taking care of our homes is something we all must do, but how we do it makes all the difference between cultivating peace and creating more chaos. What's the determining factor? The standards we are trying to live up to.

The world's standards are built upon striving: that never-ceasing belief that there's always a need to update, improve, or otherwise make better. All we have to do is stand in a grocery store line and read all the magazine headlines: "Make Your Small Space Beautiful!" "3 Easy Steps to Create the Perfect Closet!" "Easy Updates for Any Room!" Or, turn on the television to become inundated with ads for remodeling companies, shows about do-it-yourself projects that transform a house from a mess into a masterpiece, and tell us how easy it is to make our homes look beautiful with "The Lowest Prices of the Season!" Walking into any store is a full-on assault of how we *need* to decorate our homes for *every* holiday with all the greatest new looks for this year.

In addition to striving to keep up with the latest trends and updates is the ever-present fear of bacteria, germs, and stained laundry to battle against. "Good home-keepers" never have germy bathrooms or sticky kitchen counters, always have clean, stain-free clothes for their children, and can move any table-top object without fear of seeing a dust mark. There are so many "easy-to-use" products out there that the message has become "how could you not have a clean house…it's so convenient to clean nowadays!"

Uugghh. How on earth are we supposed to receive God's peace with huge piles of laundry, dust and cobwebs in the corners, messy counters, and outdated fixtures? The messages that we are at fault and a failure as a housekeeper if we are actually living with that kind of home are loud and incessant. Add to that the residual effects from the way you may have been raised to care for your home: the old *false* adage that "cleanliness is next to Godliness" or that a "clean home is a happy home," and the potential for chaos is huge.

None of this is what God intended to become of us when He blessed us with the homes we have. Our homes were meant to be a safe place for the people living in them to learn to live in grace as they grow into the people God intended for them to be. It's the relationships within the home that do that, the building itself is merely the place it can happen. If our focus is on making a house look beautiful so it fits *our ideal* of a home, we miss out on the fact that it's the love within it that makes it a home, not the furnishings, organized closets, or throw-away decorations.

The hardest push comes from our own minds: we look around at our friends' homes or at images on social media and assume that we have to live up to those standards. Yet, instead of cultivating peace, comparison steals it and places us on a never-ending treadmill of keeping up that we were never meant to pursue. Comparison kills. It assumes that we are all supposed to do the same things, keep our houses the same way, and live like one another without regard for the uniqueness of our own personal situations.

Even Scripture can be used to cause us to strive, can't it? One Biblical woman in particular has been used by the enemy to stir envy and build resentment. Consider the following selection of Scripture (Proverbs 31: 10-31 NLT):

The Wife of Noble Character

[10]Who can find a virtuous and capable wife? She is more precious than rubies. [11]Her husband can trust her, and she will greatly enrich his life. [12]She brings him good, not harm, all the days of her life. [13]She finds wool and flax and busily spins it. [14]She is like a merchant's ship, bringing her food from afar. [15]She gets up before dawn to prepare breakfast for her household and plan the day's work for her servant girls. [16]She goes to inspect a field and buys it; with her earnings she plants a vineyard. [17]She is energetic and strong, a hard worker. [18]She makes sure her dealings are profitable; her lamp burns late into the night. [19]Her hands are busy spinning thread, her fingers twisting fiber. [20]She extends a helping hand to the poor and opens her arms to the needy. [21]She has no fear of winter for her household, for everyone has warm clothes. [22]She makes

her own bedspreads. She dresses in fine linen and purple gowns. [23]Her husband is well known at the city gates, where he sits with the other civic leaders. [24]She makes belted linen garments and sashes to sell to the merchants. [25]She is clothed with strength and dignity, and she laughs without fear of the future. [26]When she speaks, her words are wise, and she gives instructions with kindness. [27]She carefully watches everything in her household and suffers nothing from laziness. [28]Her children stand and bless her. Her husband praises her: [29]"There are many virtuous and capable women in the world, but you surpass them all!" [30]Charm is deceptive, and beauty does not last; but a woman who fears the Lord will be greatly praised. [31]Reward her for all she has done. Let her deeds publicly declare her praise.

What are your initial reactions to the Wife of Noble Character described in these verses? Were you envious? Jealous? Fearful? Clearly the woman written about in these verses has many good qualities. She inspires confidence in her husband which means she is trustworthy. (v. 11) She encourages and supports him. (v. 12) She works eagerly at her tasks. (v. 13) She offers her family variety. (v. 14) She takes care of all in her home. (v. 15) She thinks before she acts and plans ahead. (vs. 16, 18, 21, 26) She takes personal responsibility for her family and herself. (vs. 19, 21-22, 26) And she is respected by others for her works and behaviors. (vs.10-11, 20, 23, 24, 28)

When I was first introduced to the "Proverbs 31 Woman" I immediately despised and envied her. She had everything I wanted and I didn't know how she could be so lucky as to have it all when there I was trying so hard to be just like her and not feeling like I was making any progress at all. Because she was in the Bible I believed she was the standard I was supposed to live up to, but I had no idea how to do all she did. I could barely keep my house picked up let alone spin thread, help the poor, run a business, and live so that my children would call me blessed. Guilt and shame poured themselves all over me.

It is unfortunate that these verses have become the source of so much chaos. The enemy exists to *"steal, kill and destroy,"* even using Scripture against us to do it, and this particular selection seems to play right into his hands. How on earth are we to do all she does? It is when we compare our current lives to what looks like "having it all" that these verses can cause us to second-guess our own home keeping.

But, look closer. This woman is the physical representation of what our lives can look like when we trust God to lead us in running our own households instead of trying to manage them in our own strength. All those fears we have about not measuring up to the standard we have adopted as truth are proved false in these verses. Instead, these verses reveal that peace in the home is not about striving to achieve a standard; it's about submitting to God, listening to the guidance of the Holy Spirit, and treating others, including the affairs of our household, as Jesus would.

When we look closely at the Wife of Noble Character we see she is revered most because of how she *treats* her household and those in her family, not by what she does. What's most important to God is creating a safe, loving environment for those who live in it, and that does not require the newest trends, seasonal decorations, or constant cleanliness.

Another battle between trust in God and trust in our own ideas is played out in the Bible in the story of Martha and Mary. Martha, sister to Mary, assumed everyone should do their fair share in preparing food for their guests rather than spending time with them. However, spending time taking care of preparations instead of spending time with others is not the way Jesus would cultivate peace within our homes:

"This woman is the physical representation of what our lives can look like when we trust God to lead us in running our own households instead of trying to manage them in our own strength."

"As Jesus and the disciples continued on their way to Jerusalem, they came to a certain village where a woman named Martha welcomed him into her home. Her sister, Mary, sat at the Lord's feet, listening to what he taught. But Martha was distracted by the big dinner she was preparing. She came to Jesus and said, "Lord, doesn't it seem unfair to you that my sister just sits here while I do all the work? Tell her to come and help me."

But the Lord said to her, "My dear Martha, you are worried and upset over all these details! There is only **one thing** worth being concerned about. Mary has discovered it, and it will not be taken away from her." (Luke 10:38-42, NLT)

The *"one thing worth being concerned about"* is Jesus: trusting Him with all the details, moving when He directs, and relying on His timing and strength. He was trying to tell Martha that when she put Him first, the rest of the details would fall into place. Mary knew her responsibilities were to prepare the meal for the guests, but she chose to listen to Jesus first. Martha chose to put the responsibilities before Jesus. According to Jesus, Mary chose what was better.

If we look at Martha we see unrest; one woman fighting God's will instead of embracing it. Jesus wanted Martha to rest *with* Him, not make preparations. I believe He would have made sure there was enough food for everyone had she let Him do so for her. We can look at her and shake our heads in judgment, but we do the same. We work in our own strength to make sure that everything will be done according to our way, instead of resting in Jesus and allowing Him to provide for us. When we do this we participate in the unrest we resent within our homes. We add to the strife. We embrace the struggle to keep up with an irrelevant standard.

I believe this is an area full of weeds for us whose roots are the impossible standards our culture dictates. Social media, Pinterest, HGTV, and the cultural inundation of constantly needing to update our homes to the freshest looks, as well as thousands of "perfectly easy" cleaning products, have woven the standard that a good home is one that's always beautifully decorated and clean. Add to this the belief that a good "housekeeper" (i.e. us) is *always* the well-prepared hostess, and it is easy to feel overwhelmed and guilt-ridden when we don't fit the standard. The problem with this standard, however, is that it is false. It breeds resentment—either at ourselves because we just can't do it all, or at everyone else in our homes for invariably messing it all up simply by living in it. It also reinforces the "keeping up with the Jones'" mentality which has its own implications both with contentment and financial responsibility.

Instead, seeking to cultivate a peace-filled *home* over a perfect *house* is where I believe Jesus leads us. We can choose to allow God to begin the process of cultivating peace in our homes, and it starts when we decide to let go of focusing on creating the perfect house. As with the relationships in our lives, cultivating peace within our homes follows a process. While understandably different than with people, this process includes several elements we have already discussed:

- Submit to God's plan for peace and order within our homes.

- Allow the Holy Spirit to guide us in how and when to pursue that plan.

- Remove the lies we have been living under about taking care of our homes and replace them with God's Truth.

- Respect our personal management style in keeping our households, without comparing what that looks like for anyone else.

God wants to create peace within our homes for us. His standards have nothing to do with the world; cultivating peace at home centers on loving well the people within that home and out of that love taking care of the home He blessed us with according to His direction. When we study the Wife of Noble Character through this lens we see that she focused on taking care of those living within her home first. Then she took care of the home itself. She made sure everyone had a variety to eat, not that the pantry was constantly stocked with everyone's favorite foods. She made sure everyone had enough oil in the lamps, not that they had a particular kind of lamp. She focused on what they needed to live a life that reflected God, not her own capabilities.

Instead of comparing ourselves with others, or even some standard of perfection we create for ourselves, the Bible continues to instruct us with this advice: *"Better a dry crust eaten in peace than a house filled with feasting—and conflict."* (Proverbs 17:1 NLT) It is better to keep things simple enough to maintain the relationships in our homes than to complicate them and create quarrels by trying to achieve an impossible standard. As always, what this looks like in your home will surely differ from what it looks like in mine, but learning to let God direct my steps in maintaining my home has made home-keeping so much more enjoyable than serving some impossible standard. Looking back, I can see now that my efforts to be perfect not only caused undue fighting between the people I hold most dear and me, but also actually made those who entered my home more uncomfortable than at ease. How could they relax when I was

> "...cultivating peace at home centers on loving well the people within that home and out of that love taking care of the home He blessed us with according to His direction."

constantly cleaning up after everyone, making sure everything remained perfect, and further reinforcing an unsustainable standard when I was able to "pull it all off?"

God will direct our steps in creating and maintaining peace within our homes if we choose to ask for His help and commit to *trying* to follow Him. (Grace covers a multitude of mistakes along the way. It's our heart God's after.) There will be seasons when keeping our homes up will have no real priority in our lives; times when maintaining a certain standard is no longer possible or even advisable. Examples of this include after a baby is born, when someone is sick, or even when one of our close relationships is struggling to survive.

During these times, instead of stressing out trying to keep up, we can let go and let God work out all things for us. The key is not to assume control over how, when, or even what keeping our homes is supposed to look like. *"O Eternal One, I know our lives are in Your hands. It is not in us to direct our own steps—we need You."* (Jeremiah 10:23 the VOICE) Cultivating peace in a home is the result of being in harmony with God's order for all things. It does not come from achieving it all in our own strength, in our own timing, or in our own way.

Our God is a god of order. If we allow him to be the Leader of our lives, we can be assured that we will have an ordered home as a result. We will be given the time to care for our homes when we keep our priorities in the right place. There is a way to cultivate peace within your home, and just like everything else, *it is a process*. Let go of the standard you are currently trying to achieve, no matter how practical it looks, and ask God to direct your steps instead. He may make changes, and He may not. What will be different is the peace that remains in your heart no matter what your home looks like.

For those of us who have a "Type A" always-have-to-be-clean-and-neat streak, this can be a very difficult step. I love having a clean, well-organized home. Looking back, though, I see that doing it in my own strength and on my own timing was sabotaging the very relationships I held most dear. Instead of playing with my children, I was constantly cleaning up after and around them, fearful of what someone might think if they came and visited. Instead of relaxing on the couch with my husband after dinner, I was cleaning the kitchen (and growing resentful that he wasn't helping) so it would be perfect again simply because I wanted it that way. Instead of enjoying my friends when they were over, I was always cleaning up before the party ended. What a waste of valuable relationship-building time!

Now, after several years of learning to trust God's way, things are improving. I am able to focus on my kids rather than cleaning up after them (even as teenagers they are just as messy!) because I know that anyone who comes over will not mind. I can let the dishes sit in the sink until morning and spend time with my husband, knowing I will be given enough time the next morning to take care of them. I can enjoy the party now because I know there will be help to clean up after it. How do I know this? I have lived it. I have asked God to help me have peace in my home through doing things His way instead of my own. Then I took a step of faith. I have trusted God to show me how to have a peace-filled home and He has been faithful. He has let me see for myself that guests care more about my state of mind than a clean home.

He has shown me that my house will be taken care of when I prioritize developing relationships instead of cleaning. He has shown me in unexpected ways that when I serve others in my home, any preparations and clean-up will be taken care of. He longs to show you how His ways can work for you, too.

Choosing to let God direct my steps in order to receive the peace He had for me in the chaos of my home was not easy because I was living with so many lies tied to fear: fear of being seen as a failure, fear of being imperfect, and fear of somehow disappointing my husband as a stay-at-home mom. Once I confronted the fears I was living with and chose to let God have control, He showed me several things that needed to change in order to have peace in my home.

First, He changed my heart. I had been so focused on how much I thought I had to do that I completely missed the fact that *He had blessed* me with a home to shelter my family and me. He had given us a place where we could be safe, learn how to live with grace and acceptance, and engage in community with others. It wasn't about how beautiful a house looked inside or out, but rather how well we were able to create an environment *in our home* where we could love each other that was most important. Once my perceptions changed, it became clear that my home was not more important than Him, my personal nourishment, my husband, or my children and family. That's why we focus on developing those relationships *before* we talk about cultivating peace within our homes.

Next, He showed me that cultivating peace was more about creating processes and routines than running around taking care of everything on my own. I had spent so many years doing everything because to let someone else do it their way or

> "I had spent so many years doing everything because to let someone else do it their way or on their timetable made me freak out."

on their timetable made me freak out. (Would it get done in time and in the right way?) While this seemed to calm the outward chaos, it only created more in my own heart as bitterness at not getting help or having to do it all began to take over. Letting God lead me in taking care of our home didn't mean He had a better way for *me* to do it all, but that He had a plan to include others in my home. Learning to let go of my own expectations in order to allow my children and husband to do things their way has been difficult...but worth it. I have learned to relax and my family has learned how to take care of *their* home instead of allowing someone else to do it for them.

Lastly, He showed me the importance of paying attention to the seasons of our family. There have been times when there is just no time to clean and others where there has been time to do a thorough purging. Peace comes when my behavior remains flexible to the season our family is in instead of an all-or-nothing mentality. As I began to trust He would provide the strength and the wisdom I needed to not only cultivate peace within my home but also within me, the chaos began to settle down.

It is this last step that has allowed me to try out different strategies. While I certainly do not believe I am an expert on creating and running a peace-filled home at all times, there are some practical tips I can share with you that might help you get started. Remember this is a process and change will take time. True also is that what has worked for me may not work for you and that is totally fine. The most amazing part of allowing God to cultivate peace within your home is growing closer to God as you let *Him* guide you, instead of me or anyone else.

1. Pray for wisdom in understanding the standard you have been trying to achieve in taking care of your home. It is important to remove any weeds in this area so that you can move forward in Truth.

2. Sit down individually with those who live in your home and ask what helps them feel the most peace-filled at home (remember to include yourself in the discussion). Once you have the data, sit together (as age allows) and work out how you can accomplish this together. For example, if your husband would like things calm when he walks through the door, ask him to call you when he is 30 minutes out so that you can prepare for him to be home. If there are certain rooms you would like organized differently, work together to determine who, how, and when that will get done. If your child wants to have his own space to do homework, discuss ways you can clear out a small area for him together. Remember, peace within a home is achieved best through treating others as more important than the home itself.

3. *Try* to do a thorough clean out of every room in the house once a year. This includes all junk drawers, closets, dressers, cubbies, etc. It also includes the attic, basement, and garage. DO NOT do this all at once!

Take one room at a time, depending on what is going on in your life, your husband's life, and the lives of your children. If you only get to a few rooms, you will be better off than not doing any at all. Then, as part of cleaning out each room, create a system of keeping it that way. Do you need paper trays for each family member in the office area so papers aren't lying all over the place? Do the kids need a lower cabinet for their plates and cups so they can help you put the dishes away? Does the garage need pegs and storage bins so that toys and stored items are out of the way?

4. Tired of running to the store every day, or not having what you need when you need it? Consider getting in the habit of making a weekly meal menu and grocery list, and then planning a trip to the grocery store (and other places for household supplies) only once a week. My menu plan includes dinner meals only, but you can do it to include lunch, breakfast, and snacks. Focus on the foods and ingredients you use regularly. Also, remember to check your supplies so you can replace what is running low. Use the weekly ad of your favorite store to plan your menu and to stock up on sale items you use regularly. You can also subscribe to on-line services that produce menus and grocery lists for you and even deliver food to your front door.

5. Get in the habit of looking at your menu each morning to be sure you defrost what's needed, and

set aside enough time before your scheduled eating time to prepare it without being rushed. Consider making this time an event for you and your family. Including music, an appetizer (snack), and/or drinks (juice, etc.) while you are preparing the meal can help to calm any impatience as well as bring your family closer. Or, consider using a Crockpot so your meal is complete when you walk in the door from a long day. (Bonus: most recipes do not require defrosting the main ingredients!)

6. Assign daily and weekly tasks to your children. These can be regularly assigned tasks or assigned depending on your needs. Even young children can be taught how to empty a small trash bin, put clothes in their drawers, and pick up toys. Focus on not how perfectly the job is done, but on training them to be responsible members of the family.

7. Have a set of cleaning wipes in every bathroom, as well as extra plastic bags for trash. That way you can do a quick clean-up when you have an unexpected minute.

8. Consider ditching a regular cleaning routine and doing things around the house as needed. If the floor is dirty and you have the time at the moment, mop it. If a carpet needs vacuuming, do it if you can right then. Wipe down a bathroom while the kids are in the bath and rinse out the tub when you are finished. The point here is this: People and relationships are more important than cleaning your home. When we

let go of the control over cleaning our homes and allow God to show us when the right time is to do something, we become more able to keep up with them. Remember, He is a God of order, and He knows about germs, bacteria, and sickness. If you are asking Him for help, He will show you.

9. Begin a new load of laundry each morning before work, transferring it to the dryer when you come home (or training your children to do this, especially for their own laundry as they get older). As you (or others) fold the clothes, place them in piles according to each person and even by drawer/space. (I fold all my husband's shirts in one pile, his pants in another, etc.) Have each child put away their own clothes before they go to bed.

10. Create a weekly errand schedule around the activities you have to do outside of your house. For instance, if you have to go to your child's ballet class, plan to do whatever errands you can that are in the same place as, or on the way to/from, the class. If you go to the grocery store, Target, and a local mall regularly, set up your schedule so you only go once a week. This will do two things for you; give you more time, and save you money.

11. Consider having a daily quiet time in your house where everyone is in their rooms either sleeping or relaxing quietly at the same time (not at bedtime). This serves several purposes. You have some regular down time. The kids learn how to entertain them-

selves. And, it can offer a nice transition time from one stage of the day to the next.

12. Set a time limit on the screens in your home for yourself. Facebook, Pinterest, and Instagram, while fun and entertaining, can be a huge drain on the time we have each day. Also, consider eliminating your name from unnecessary store lists and set your filter to "extremely high" so only e-mails from people you know end up in your inbox. Then, check your junk box only once in a while to make sure someone you know isn't in there. The point isn't to eliminate, but to live in a balance of how we are using our time each day.

13. Plan ahead for extra projects you are going to be doing in your house. For example, if you are going to organize the kitchen, plan ahead for it by clearing off your schedule, getting tasks and chores regularly done at that time rescheduled for different times, and making sure you have all you need before you start. The same goes for landscaping projects, painting, and other household projects.

14. Consider purchasing those things for your home that make you feel peaceful. Scented candles, relaxing music, organizational tools; whatever helps you (and anyone else in your home) feel more peace in your home. If you have what you need to feel peace-filled, chances are your family will feel peace and relax too.

15. Prayerfully consider whether the home you are currently living in is the one God wants you to stay in. Could the chaos in your home be alleviated by downsizing or relocating?

Please remember that these are only suggestions and ideas for you to consider. Always begin with asking God to direct your steps and then take that step of faith. He won't let you down! The most important thing to remember is God *wants* to create a peace-filled home *for* you!

Let's Pray

Father God, thank You for providing a home for us and our families. Thank You for a roof over our heads and a place where we can learn and grow and love. Please give us wisdom in how to best take care of it according to Your will. Reveal to us the false standards we may be living with so that we may learn to trust You instead. Help us to love well the people inside our homes and keep us from placing too high a value on the image of our homes. In Jesus' name, Amen.

Pay careful attention to your own work, for then you will get the satisfaction of a job well done, and you won't need to compare yourself to anyone else. For we are each responsible for our own conduct.

Galatians 6:4-5 NLT

Chapter Eight

Cultivating Peace in Work

"Work willingly at whatever you do, as though you were working for the Lord rather than for people. Remember that the Lord will give you an inheritance as your reward, and that the Master you are serving is Christ."

Colossians 3:23-24 NLT

Eight

Over the years, I have noticed one area of women's lives that seems to cause more chaos than others: working.

I grew up believing that a woman who had a career *and* took care of her family was the pinnacle of success. What mattered was getting a good education, advancing in a career, and contributing to the family finances. Choosing to stay at home with our future children was never a viable option for me: being a good mom (to me) meant that I modeled how to have it all for our children.

Before our children were born I was well on my way to becoming a successful educator. I advanced in my career rapidly, earning the respect of my colleagues and the trust of my supervisors. I was given more responsibilities (a good thing in the teaching world as it makes you harder to replace when there are cutbacks) and asked to lead several committees and projects. My salary rose as well; for a while my husband and I contributed almost equally to our family's finances. I loved going to work every day; I was a natural at teaching and found total fulfillment in it.

After the birth of my first child, my plans to continue working began to unravel. I was eager to prove I could have it all, only to discover how wrong I had been. The standard I had

> "I wanted to be a good stay-at-home mom, but the monotony and simplicity bored me to tears. I longed for significance, to live a life that mattered."

set for myself as a teacher constantly battled the standards I was trying to set for myself as a mom. I entered into every day believing I wasn't good enough because I couldn't be the great teacher I wanted to be without feeling like I wasn't being a good mom, and I couldn't be the great mom I wanted to be without feeling like I was not putting enough effort into my students. I couldn't figure out what I was doing "wrong." All of the other women I knew were working and had children and seemed to have it all together, why couldn't I be more like them?

After I moved to South Carolina and became a stay-at-home mom the battle of standards was still there, only differently. I had no idea what I was doing. I had spent over a decade as a teacher, which didn't prepare me at all to be a mom. What was I to do with all the skills and talents I had developed? Additionally I now wasn't contributing to our family's finances so I began to feel as if I was no longer an equal partner in our marriage. Where I was once connected and challenged as an educator with my colleagues, I didn't fit with all the other stay-at-home moms I was meeting: they seemed to be able to navigate all the challenges of motherhood with ease and had a genuine desire to be at home. I seemed to never get it right and had never contemplated even wanting to be at home with my kids.

Once we began homeschooling our children and I began

writing and speaking, the battle of standards shifted yet again. I wasn't a "working mom" because I didn't get paid, I wasn't a "real" stay-at-home mom because I didn't participate in all the school-based activities, and I didn't fit the mold of the traditional homeschooling mom because I was also a speaker and writer.

I wanted to be a good stay-at-home mom, but the monotony and simplicity bored me to tears. I longed for significance, to live a life that mattered, but heading back to work was not something my husband's schedule allowed for. I was living in the chaos of the proverbial debate: to work or not to work, and it was making me nuts.

The debate over whether or not to work outside the home once we have children has plagued women since the time we began entering the workforce. We have struggled to prove we have the gifts, talents, and skills to do the jobs we want to pursue in our lives. We have had to justify staying home instead of pursuing a career. We have had to endure judgment from other women on both sides of the argument.

How then do we cultivate peace in this area filled with so much chaos from not only within ourselves but from the outside world as well? We know we are called to minister to others. *Each one should use whatever gift he has received to serve others, faithfully administering God's grace in its various forms.*

> "God's peace doesn't come when we have our lives all worked out and organized. It comes in the messes of living every day in the present of what we have today."

(1Peter 4:10) However, it is not specified that we can only carry out this mandate in a paying job. Deuteronomy 11:18-21 indicates a responsibility to teach our children, but it is not clear whether that precludes working outside the home. Yet, even the Proverbs 31 woman worked at tasks other than taking care of her children and home.

Making the decision to work outside the home or not is personal. Finances, career options, partnership within the marriage, and circumstances within our families all need to be taken into account. Therefore, *there should be no debate over whether or not a woman should work outside the home. I believe that is a decision to be made solely between God, your husband (if you are married), and you.* What's important to remember is that there is no perfect scenario:

"There's just no perfect scenario. The moms I know who went back to work after their six-week maternity leave felt like they had been robbed of something. The moms who took on the lion's share of classroom volunteering and playdate hosting felt like they were missing out on grown-up life. *Their* grown up life. So is it just all bad? No, it's all good."[47]

Why is it that this debate still even exists? Because we keep thinking there is some "perfect" way we can make it all work. We keep thinking that if we could just figure out how to make everything we want to do in a day fit, so that we can do it all and feel like we are doing it all well, then we could trust that our choices were right. Only it's not about any of that and it never has been. There is no RIGHT way. There is no perfection to be achieved. God's peace doesn't come when we have our lives all worked out and organized. It comes in the messes of living every day in the present of what we have today.

We seem to need permission to live our lives one decision at a time, messy and imperfectly, longing for more but not knowing how to get there. It's as if permission would make it OK and then we could let down the burden we carry around full of worry and fear and doubt. Well, here's permission: You are free to live the best life you can with what you have right now.

If you are a single mom you are off the hook to be both parents and make sure you are everything your children need. If you are a stay-at-home mom you are off the hook to have to be busy all the time so it doesn't seem you are "wasting" your life. If you are in the marketplace you are off the hook to have to balance making everything from scratch to being perfectly coiffed for work. But this is not *my* permission, I am no one. This is permission from God Himself to stop comparing your life to anyone else's and instead enjoy what He has given you. *It's the comparison that kills our joy and steals our peace.*

Working moms compare their hectic schedules to what they think a stay-at-home mom's life is like and believe they are falling short. Stay-at-home moms look at working moms in wonder of how they keep it all together, comparing their messy life to what they think is a better one. Single moms fear they aren't enough for their kids. ALL of us are not enough. ALL of us struggle and make mistakes and never feel as if we are living up to the standards we have adopted as truth. Can we please just stop?

You are unique. Your situation is unique. You can be used by God no matter what your life looks like. It may be through your kids. It may be in how you treat your clients. It may be in how you interact with other women, or treat those you come in contact with in the worlds in which you move.

- If you are a single mom you *can* receive God's peace in working as much as you have to when you accept His standards for your life. You are not enough, but He is and He wants to help. Will you trust Him?

- If you are at home you *can* receive God's peace in the never ending need when you accept His standards for your life. You are not enough, but He is and He wants to help. Will you trust Him?

- If you are in the marketplace you *can* receive God's peace in the multitude of decisions and schedules you manage when you to accept His standards for your life. You are not enough, but He is and he wants to help you too. Will you trust Him?

When we choose to trust that God knows exactly where we are and that He is working on our behalf to move us closer to Him, one day at a time, we can look at our lives and assess the discontent we feel. Are we happy? If not, why not? Is it because we want to live a life different from the one we are living? What are the motives behind that desire? If you are financially strapped and not working, maybe it is time to seek employment. If you are in a job that causes more chaos than the financial benefit, maybe it's time to leave. I have no idea what decision you should make, but I know that God's peace follows choices that seek to honor Him.

So, what exactly is causing your chaos? Sit in that awhile, because it matters.

All of what I have written comes down to this chapter:

We are free, forever, from ever being condemned for not being enough. When that realization begins to take shape, the debate over whether or not a woman should work outside the home dies. We are all created in the image of God to do something with the life we have been given. We all have influence that is meant to lift others up and show them the way to Jesus. It may come as a stay-at-home mom

"All of what I have written comes down to this chapter: We are free, forever, from ever being condemned for not being enough."

or working mom, married woman or single woman. When we stop comparing, and stop using our own standards as the "right" way to live, we begin to use our influence for good.

Imagine what life could be like if we championed each other in the work we do, encouraging each other that God will step in and fill the gaps we all feel? What could happen to you if you were encouraged by other women in the marketplace, at home, and in ministry, whether single or married? What could happen if YOU chose to be one of those women too?

To work or not to work isn't the question we should be asking in cultivating peace in work. What we should be asking is how we can best use what we have been given without worrying over whether it is enough or looks like everyone else.

Receiving God's peace in the work we do has nothing to do with the actual work itself. It's in how we view that work. How we view that work is dependent upon the expectations we have. The chaos I experienced as a teacher after I became a mom was due to the fact that I had standards that were so high there was no reaching them. Since I believed I wasn't enough I always felt like I was failing. That wasn't the case at all, but because I *felt* like it was I lived like it was; always trying to be better in everything I was doing. When I left teaching I experienced chaos because I had standards again that were exceedingly high and I could never reach them. Again, feelings of failure reigned because I never felt like I was enough and againI always tried to be better.

I received God's peace when I stopped running after my own standards (and the world's, and even of those around me). I chose to ignore all the voices telling me I was supposed to stay home, those telling me I was supposed to go back to work, and those telling me I could never be good enough like the women doing what I wasn't doing. I want so much for you to do the same.

When we choose to look at how we spend our days as an opportunity to use the gifts and talents we have been given for the work we have right now, whether it is that of mom, career woman, or both, we are given the opportunity to experience a new level of freedom. In that freedom, there is peace. It doesn't come from a better job, more time with our kids, or a balanced life. It comes from opening our tight fists and releasing all the fears, worries, hopes and dreams we have and embracing what's right in front of us instead.

"Commit everything you do to the Lord. Trust him, and he will help you. Be still in the presence of the Lord, and wait patiently for him to act."

Psalm 37: 5, 7 NLT

God knows what you need. God knows what you want. Peace comes in trusting that where He has you right now is not where you will stay, calm or chaotic. You will have a valley. You will have a peak. You will experience the climb and descent over and over until you meet Jesus. Embrace it all, reminding yourself as often as you need that you are choosing to trust that God is in control and has good things in store for you that you can yet imagine well enough to even be able to ask Him for.

"No matter where you spend your time each day, one thing is certain: you have been given influence and the gifts and talents necessary for leveraging that influence."

No matter where you spend your time each day, one thing is certain: you have been given influence and the gifts and talents necessary for leveraging that influence. Whether in a paid career or not, your influence is no less valuable. I have come to believe that the chaos we experience comes not from whether or not we work outside the home, but whether or not we are using the influence we have been given in a way that honors God.

If you are in a relationship with Jesus Christ and seeking God's will, the issue is not whether or not to work outside the home, but rather being willing to follow where He is leading. The important thing is to let God direct our steps. If we have no peace in our hearts, our marriages, or our family as a result of the work we are doing (whether inside the home only, or outside the home as well), it is up to us to *choose* to seek out God's guidance as to whether or not we should continue. If making a career change is in the plans for the garden God is cultivating in you, you will be able to find peace in that decision. This does not mean you won't experience fear or anxiety. Sometimes we have to go where we feel the most peace, even if it is the option that presents the least chaos. You could be a career-oriented woman who feels called to stay at home or a stay-at-home mom who feels called to go back to work. Either way, you will experience growing levels of His peace when you keep your priorities in order, including submitting to God's will for where and when to work.

Being miserable in our work may be an indication that we have at least one weed growing in that part of our gardens. Many times it is the weed of fear of the unknown. *What would I do if I didn't stay in this job? Will my children be all right without me if I enter into a job outside the home? Will our family's finances remain stable if I stay home?* These doubts and fears are meant to block us from seeking and following God's will. Instead of listening to them, as followers of Christ we can bring any fears or doubts we may have to God and ask Him to help sort out the weeds from the truth. So often we are deceived by the lies that tell us if we leave a career we will never be able to return, or that if we leave our homes we will never be able to be with our children again. This is where trust and a sense of peace play an important role. Will we trust God enough to wait for His direction? Will we seek the decision that allows us to receive His peace?

God not only has a plan, but a specific timing for His plan as well. I left a career, but it doesn't mean I will never have one again. It simply may not be part of His plan for me at this time. The same is true for you. You may have a great career right now which works peacefully with your relationship with God, your husband, and your family. In this, staying at home may not be part of His plan for you at this time. You may be staying at home and have the same result. When you wait on God and follow His peace in making the decision to work outside the home or not, the rest of the areas of your life will work in harmony with each other. This doesn't mean there will not still be conflict (we are all human after all), but there will be peace as we learn to trust and depend on God. I am, and always will be, an advocate for women to trust in God above all else, including whether or not they should pursue a career in addition to or other than motherhood. *When you allow God to be in control of your life, there is no wrong or poor choice, only His plan for you.*

The question now before us is this: how do we cultivate peace around us when we are maneuvering through the world? The answer lies in the same process of developing the four key principles of developing relationships (submission, respect, forgiveness, and intimacy) that we have been learning to operate under in all other areas of our lives. The focus is not so much about whether or not we work outside of the home, but how we handle ourselves within the situations we find ourselves on a daily basis. In the home and out, we are to submit to those God has placed in positions of authority over us, offer respect to those we interact with, forgive those who cause us harm, and allow Jesus to shine His light on those around us, *through us.* In the context of employment, we are to submit to the authority of our employer, offer them and our colleagues respect, extend (and ask for where appropriate) forgiveness for any wrongdoings, and seek to build relationships in order to bring the love of Jesus into our workplace.

Much of the angst we may feel in our daily work could be due to missing one or more key principles of the process of developing relationships. If we are missing one or more of these key principles in any of our core relationships (with God, ourselves, our husbands (if married) and our children and within our family), the resulting chaos we are living with affects our perspective on what we do. This is why I believe God has an order to cultivating peace within our lives: our work (whether it's within the home or without, or both) can be less chaotic when we have begun to work through the process (not achieved perfection) in the core relationships we have in our lives. When we are submitted to God's authority and plan for our lives, our work becomes less about us and more about those we are serving.

If we operate from the premise that any job we have, from in the home to in the workplace, is part of God's plan for us, then choosing to submit to His sovereign authority in this area of our lives is the first step in allowing Him to cultivate more peace within us as we work. This includes submitting to those He places in authority over us from our husbands (when we work in our homes) to our employers (when we work outside of the home). Remember, we are placing our ultimate trust in God Himself. He is in control and knows any situation we find ourselves in.

Second, we can receive more of His peace when we choose to offer respect to those around us in our workplace. At home, this is cultivated within the process I introduced with our husbands and children. Within the marketplace, this can be cultivated when you see your employer and fellow employees as God's creation, complete with sinful natures that often lead them astray, just as we have been. Offering them respect doesn't mean we have to agree or invite them to be a part of our lives. It means we value them because God does, whether or not they are living a life that honors Him.

Third, a deeper peace is cultivated when we choose to forgive as we have been forgiven. We make mistakes. Our husbands and children make mistakes. Our employers, colleagues, and clients make mistakes. Offering forgiveness costs us nothing, but in doing so we receive freedom from anger, resentment, and bitterness. Without those negative emotions burdening our hearts, we can receive more of God's love for ourselves and others which can result in more peace in any situation.

Lastly, when we live authentic lives we let the light of peace that we have been cultivating within us help us to build relationships (intimacy) with co-workers and colleagues (just as we have been doing with our husbands, children, and families). We do not have to live "perfect" lives in order to bring glory to God. On the contrary, I believe we are most effective as beacons of hope when we appropriately share our stories of brokenness, crisis of faith, and struggles in the context of trying to trust God with all of it.

The reality of the Christ-centered life is that they are

often just as messy, difficult, and painful as any other life. Offering transparency in how we are trying to allow God's strength to carry us through these times does more to further the gospel than hiding everything away. Living our lives transparently, unafraid of sharing the good, the bad and the ugly, shows how God loves us, not how we rescue ourselves. In a world searching for answers, an authentic Christian, who meets others where they are in order to share how far God can take them, does more to show the love of Christ than one who hides behind a façade.

No matter where we spend our time each day, this process can guide us in receiving God's peace no matter how chaotic our circumstances. As God cultivates more peace within us, we can more authentically love, which is the hallmark of the Christian faith.

"If you remain in me and my words remain in you,
ask whatever you will, and it will be given you.
This is to my father's glory, that you bear much fruit,
showing yourselves to be my disciples. My command
is this: Love each other as I have loved you."

(John 15:7-8, 12, NIV)

• • •

Does cultivating this seed of peace, along with balancing all the others we have planted, sound like too much to do? In our own strength it is, but with God in control, nothing is too impossible to accomplish. We all have the same amount of time in any given day; the difference between having a peacefilled day and a hectic one is in remembering God is in control. When you begin your day with God, allowing Him to fill you with the strength, wisdom, and energy needed for that day, you then allow Him to guide you through the millions of actions, reactions, and decisions you make in order to continue cultivating peace.

One of the greatest ways I have found to learn to allow God to cultivate the seed for peace in the work I do is by developing a habit of ordering my days in a certain way. Routine has been essential for keeping my peace. From personal and family schedules to school and activities schedules, to work and play schedules, there is a lot to keep track of in a day. Simply letting each day hit you, without any advance planning or structure, is an opportunity for chaos to reign again. When we take time each week to look at the next week, we then can gain a visual picture of what's coming at us each week in order to ask God to help us develop a plan for peace before other things steal that time away. (I have used something I call a Schedule Tracker™ for years, which is available on my website, StephanieHaynes.net, as part of the Digging Deeper material under the Cultivating Peace tab.) This then cultivates peace in our work by allowing us to let go of guilt in doing the work we know God has called us to do because we know we have our priorities balanced.

> "We all have the same amount of time in any given day; the difference between having a peace-filled day and a hectic one is in remembering God is in control."

However, while there is peace in creating a routine, there is also the potential of planning ourselves into oblivion. Over-planning each day simply because you have space to fill is as bad as not planning at all. It is important to remember that despite our best planning, we often cannot foresee the curves our paths may take. All we can do is plan for what we hope will happen and then pray for God to guide our steps. This may even mean completely ditching our plans mid-day or mid-week in order to remain in God's will for the time He gives us each day. Sometimes our time will seem unbalanced, with the majority of our day spent focusing on one particular area (after the birth of a child or a change in career for example). When we use some type of planning system we can have peace in these times because we can look back and look ahead and "see" that we have either taken the time for the other areas in our life, or planned to do so in the future. In this way, the enemy can no longer plant the weeds of guilt in our work or of distraction in our family time and we can quit listening to the lying voices that try and claim we aren't getting enough done.

While this process is unique to each of us, if you have never done anything like this you may need a place to start. I take an hour or so most weekends to plan out my next week. I also use this time to plan out our weekly menu. Before I begin, I first ask my husband what his schedule will be. Then I know what nights he will be home or away and what, if anything, he needs me to do. Next I make a list of all the tasks I think need to be accomplished that week. I focus on both self-focused tasks (quiet time and self-care time) and other-focused tasks (spending time with my husband, my children, and my family) as well as what I need to do for my home and for my career. Finally, I pray and ask God to remove anything He doesn't want in my schedule, to add in anything I missed, and to guide me every step of the way.

In addition to creating a personal, God centered, regular routine, we should also allow for times when there are no "have to's." Times where we can relax, unwind, and let go of moving from one thing to another. That is one of the many benefits of having a regular Sabbath day. The Sabbath was created by God as a day of rest. *"God saw all that he had made, and it was very good. And there was evening, and there was morning—the sixth day. Thus, the heavens and the earth were completed in all their vast array. By the seventh day God had finished the work he had been doing; so on the seventh day he rested from all his work. And God blessed the seventh day and made it holy, because on it he rested from all the work of creating that he had done."* (Genesis 1:31-2:3)

The Sabbath is our day of rest too, and we *need* it. There is so much to do every day, every week, all year long. Our quiet times are meant to bring us refreshment for the day, but we need regular weekly days dedicated to just being as well. I can hear you now, "Yeah right! I have so much to do in a week, how can I do it in only six days?" I get it, really, and I believe there are seasons where trying to get everything done in six days can cause more chaos than cultivate peace.

However, have you stopped to think about that statement from God's perspective? Is what you do in a week more important than the creation of the world? I come in peace about this and mean no guilt or shame, so please hear my heart on this. Just as I have been trying to convey God's message to trust Him to cultivate peace in your daily life, I believe God wants you to hear this part as well. You need a regular, every-seventh-day Sabbath, and it can be done. Remember, I am a busy woman too, and the thought of having to do it all in six rather than seven days actually nauseated me at first.

When the idea of committing to a regular Sabbath day first seeped into my consciousness, I immediately rejected it. There was no way I could do all I was doing in only six days. My kids, who were toddlers and preschoolers at the time, need-ed me to be "on" every day. Everyone needed to eat. If I didn't pick up one day, there would be double to do the next, and there was no margin in the next day to do double-duty. The margin I had begun to create in making time to be with God and my husband and kids, to take care of myself and my home, to begin the ministry I felt God calling me to run, almost filled every waking moment in my life, and for the first time ever in my life I had tasted what true peace felt like. I didn't want to lose that feeling and trying to now do it all in only six days completely freaked me out. It seemed as if the idea of a Sabbath was everywhere I went, though, so I chose to ignore the voice of fear in order to hear what God was trying to tell me.

I read what the Bible said about the Sabbath, the most convicting scripture coming from Exodus 20:8-11a. I observed how others, including the pastors at my church, were doing it. Then I prayed and asked God to show me how.

When I was first considering trying to establish a Sabbath, I believed it was supposed to be filled with Scripture reading, prayer, and maybe even fasting. This didn't sound very enjoyable, let alone restful or peaceful to me. How would I ever be able to secure the time to focus, let alone teach my family to do the same? No. Thank. You. What I learned from Scripture and my observations though is that the purpose of the Sabbath is to rest from the work we do the rest of the week. *"By the seventh day God had finished the work he had been doing; so on the seventh day he rested from all his work."* (Genesis 2:2) Did you catch that? God Himself rested from all the work He had been doing. He rested.

> "What I learned from Scripture and my observations though is that the purpose of the Sabbath is to rest from the work we do the rest of the week."

Understanding this concept helped me understand the importance of resting from the work I did on a regular basis. Every other day of the week I did laundry, worked on educating my children, ran errands, cleaned, worked as a volunteer, and developed the skills I needed for ministry. Using my time in these ways precluded many things I enjoyed doing which helped me to rest--sleeping in, being out in nature, reading a book, or even gardening. Those things are what a Sabbath is for. True, prayer and Scripture are a part of my regular Sabbath, as they should be, but they are not the *only* thing I do. Your Sabbath can be filled with those things that bring you rest from the work you do the other six days of the week as well.

I know it is counter-cultural to feel like we actually have permission to rest and not strive to keep up or get ahead. Remember the verse that God used to grab my attention before all this started, though? It was the NIV version of Psalm 46:10: *"Be still and know that I am God."* Around the same time I began trying to develop a regular Sabbath for myself, God directed me to a different translation of the verse. The New American Standard Bible writes it this way, *"Cease striving and know that I am God."* (Psalm 46:10) *Cease striving.* God Himself is giving us permission to stop always "doing" every minute of every day and instead trust that He *is* in control.

Learning to follow God in establishing a Sabbath has been messy; there have been months where a weekly Sabbath happened and months when it didn't. The point is that my heart longs to honor God by trusting in His word and His ways, not in whether or not I perfectly execute that longing. That's what grace is all about. God knows we will try and fail, but He loves us anyway and, because of Jesus, we are forgiven and made righteous even in the mess. Choosing to trust God in order to allow Him to cultivate His peace within our lives involves living differently than the world in which we find ourselves. When we do, especially when it's one messy but courageous step of faith at a time, His light shines through us, enticing others to seek Him out through us. Imagine how others in your life could be affected by making a choice to trust God's direction in establishing a Sabbath in your own life.

One of the biggest barriers to establishing a Sabbath is not knowing when or what to do on one. Start where everything else began: with God. Take the time to first ask Him what day of the week your Sabbath should be and what it should look like. The Bible says we are to rest every seventh day (Genesis 2:3), not on every Saturday or Sunday. Although the Jews before Christ as well as modern-day Jews recognize a cultural Sabbath on Saturday, and Christians have traditionally ascribed Sundays as a cultural day of rest, holding to these specific days will not be possible for everyone.

If, for example, you are a dual-income family who has Tuesdays and Wednesdays off, does that mean that you are breaking the Sabbath if you don't rest on Saturday or Sunday? What about pastors and other church volunteers who traditionally work on Saturdays or Sundays? Are they breaking a Sabbath to preach and serve? I don't believe so. Remember, if your life is centered on God, you will be in His will no matter if you work on the weekends or not. Your Sabbath, therefore, can occur on any day of the week.

When I truly trust God to help me get everything done that He wants me to do, and let go of the rest, there is always a Sabbath. Often it is the sweetest day of my week. This can be true for you too. Like everything else you have been learning, this is a life-long process that will take time to develop, but I promise it will be worth it.

Here are a few ideas to help you get prepared:

1. Make meals ahead of time and gather paper products so you don't have to cook or do dishes.

2. Finish laundry and errands on other days, or leave it for the day after your Sabbath.

3. If there are obligations already scheduled, consider rescheduling if at all possible.

4. Discuss the idea with you family and brainstorm ways everyone can help prepare.

5. Remember that this too is a process. Some weeks it may go smoothly, and some it may not. Invite the Holy Spirit to guide you and follow where His peace is.

Here are a few ideas to consider for what to do on a Sabbath. Remember the key is to do things that bring you closer to God, not get you caught up or ahead in some way related to your "regular" life:

1. Attend church.

2. Read through a chapter of your Bible.

3. Sit and meditate on God and His word.

4. Sleep in.

5. Take a walk.

6. Visit with friends.

7. Create something new. (We all have a creative side!)

8. Garden.

9. Rest.

10. Experience nature.

11. Spend time alone.

12. Spend time with those you love.

13. Try something new.

14. Clean out a closet, room, or drawer. Cleaning out the muck often clears out space for God to move in.

15. Don't plan a thing and follow wherever God leads.

• • •

The act of learning to receive God's peace in the midst of your chaos, whether that chaos is within yourself, within one of your relationships, within your home, or within your daily work, is a life-long process. This book has been only the beginning. There is much to learn, but God… He knows right where you are this very moment. He knows your struggles, your deepest longings, and the state of your heart. He isn't standing over you in judgement, but rather is waiting for you to allow Him to step in and show you the way into His peace. That, my friend, is how we cultivate peace in our lives. May we always remember it's not up to us to make everything work out in our lives, and may we rest in the truth that He is bigger than any chaos we will ever face.

Let's Pray

Father God, I ask that you bless each of us with Your peace. I pray you shower us with Your wisdom to understand how to trust You in this season of our lives. Please move in so close that we can feel you so intimately and powerfully that that taste drives us deeper into trusting You with more and more of our lives. Please bless us in the work we do and guide us in living this life You have given us according to Your will. In Jesus' name, Amen.

"And we know that God causes everything to work together for the good of those who love God and are called according to his purpose for them. For God knew his people in advance, and he chose them to become like his Son, so that his Son would be the firstborn among many brothers and sisters."

Romans 8:28-29 NLT

Digging Deeper

Often while reading a good book I will highlight and notate in the margin any thoughts I have. My ambition is to remember what I have read, using my markings as a way to find a good place to come back to and remind myself of what I thought was important. Too often though, once I am finished with the book, it goes on my bookshelf, relegated to something I've checked off on a to-do list and I (almost) never come back to it.

This book may be like that for you, and that's fine. Maybe, however, you have had some revelation or something in a chapter has struck a nerve or made you think. I invite you to dig a little deeper. When we dig in a lot can happen. We can release pain and receive healing. We can release bitterness and receive grace. We can release fear and receive courage.

I have prepared a special guide just for you to dig a little deeper. Head on over to StephanieHaynes.net. Under the Cultivating Peace tab click the subheading for Digging Deeper. This will unlock a free, downloadable, printable pdf document that will contain reflective questions separated by chapter to take you deeper, Scripture-centered devotions to draw you closer to Jesus, and time-management tools meant to free you from the chaos that can take over our minds when we have to keep track of too much. How deep you dig is up to you, but I do know this: the deeper you allow Jesus to take you, the more peace you will feel no matter how chaotic your life may get.

May the peace of God, which transcends all under-standing, guard your heart and mind in Christ Jesus as you continue to trust Him more and more, one messy step of courageous faith at a time!

Stephanie

References

Introduction

[1] At the time I was mentored by Betsy Smith, Women's Pastor at Seacoast Church, Mt. Pleasant Campus

Chapter One

[2] http://www.gotquestions.org/abide-in-Christ.html
[3] Galatians 5:22-23 (NLT)
[4] John 1:1-5 (NLT)
[5] John 3:16-17 (NLT)
[6] Ephesians 2:1-3 (NLT)
[7] John 14:26 (NLT)
[8] 2 Corinthians 1:21-22 (NIV)
[9] John 3:16-17 (NIV)
[10] Romans 12:2 (NLT)
[11] John 14:6 (NLT)

Chapter Two

[12] The Renaissance Program is a school-wide program devoted to recognizing ALL students for academic achievement in an effort to motivate them. Students are recognized, for example, for moving from a 2.0 GPA to a 2.5 GPA, perfect attendance, no longer having F's on their report card, etc.
[13] Known as The Health Academy at Ygnacio Valley High School in Concord, California, we spent three years with the same group of students. Our graduation rate was 100% with the majority going off to college as first generation high school graduates and college attendees.
[14] Psalm 37:4 (NLT)
[15] Jeremiah 31:3 (NIV)
[16] Romans 8:38-39 (NLT)"
[17] God grant me the serenity to accept the things I cannot change; courage to change the things I can; and wisdom to know the difference. Living one day at a time; enjoying one moment at a time; accepting hardships as the pathway to peace; taking, as He did, this sinful world as it is, not as I would have it; trusting that He will make all things right if I surrender to His will; So that I may be reasonably happy in this life and supremely happy with Him forever and ever in the next. Amen.
[18] Ephesians 6:10-17 (NLT)

Chapter Three

[19] Bruce Bickel and Stan Jantz, Knowing the Bible 101, page 61-62. This is a fantastic book if you'd like to learn more about the Bible.
[20] Hebrews 11:1 (NLT)

Chapter Four

[21] Jennifer Read Hawthorne, Change Your Thoughts, Change Your World @2014: http://www.jenniferhawthorne.com/articles/change_your_thoughts.html

[22] Margaret Thatcher, http://www.goodreads.com/quotes/792731-watch-your-thoughts-for-they-will-become-actions

[23] Eleanor Roosevelt, This is My Story

[24] Ephesians 6:16 (NLT)

[25] 2 Corinthians 10:5 (NIV)

[26] 2 Corinthians 5:21 (VOICE)

[27] 1 John 4:14 (VOICE)

[28] 1 Corinthians 16:13 (NIV)

[29] Romans 12:2 (NLT)

[30] Hebrews 4:12 (VOICE)

[31] Nancy Leigh DeMoss; The Lies Women Believe, and the Truth That Sets Them Free. Chicago, Moody Publishers. 2001

[32] Bold-face headers in this section are adapted from the book the Lies Women Believe and the Truth That Sets them Free

[33] Boundaries: When to Say Yes, When to Say No to Take Control of Your Life by Dr. Henry Cloud and Dr. John Townsend in an excellent resource for this process

Chapter Five

[34] Genesis Chapter 3

[35] Genesis 17:7 (NIV)

[36] Image from https://highsteppinginheavenlyplaces.wordpress.com/2009/11/19/week-7-homework-discussion/

[37] Martha Peace, The Excellent Wife, ©1999 Focus Publishing Inc. Chapter 1, page 4

[38] Women of Faith™ Study Bible, NIV version, ©2001 by Zondervan. Page 1935

[39] John 10:10a (NIV)

[40] Romans 8:28 (NLT)

[41] Genesis 2:18 (NLT)

[42] Psalm 139:13 (NIV)

[43] John 15:9,12 (NIV)

[44] http://www.focusonthefamily.com/marriage/divorce-and-infidelity/forgiveness-and-restoration/forgiveness-what-it-is-and-what-it-isnt

Chapter Six

[45] Philippians 4:6-7 (NIV)

[46] Psalm 139: 13, 16 (NIV)

Chapter Eight

[47] The Goodbye Year, Toni Piccinini, pg 55

For more encouragement to take your next steps of courageous faith, visit Stephanie online at StephanieHaynes.net today!

The Author's Champion

28107669R00144

Made in the USA
San Bernardino, CA
20 December 2015